BETH LUEDERS

TwoDaysLonger

HOWARD
PUBLISHING CO.

DISCOVERING MORE OF GOD

AS *YOU WAIT FOR HIM*

Our purpose at Howard Publishing is to:
•*Increase faith* in the hearts of growing Christians
•*Inspire holiness* in the lives of believers
•*Instill hope* in the hearts of struggling people everywhere
Because He's coming again!

Two Days Longer © 2006 Beth Lueders
All rights reserved. Printed in the United States of America
Published by Howard Publishing Co., Inc.
3117 North Seventh Street, West Monroe, LA 71291-2227
www.howardpublishing.com
In association with the literary agency of Alive Communications, Inc.
7680 Goddard Street, Suite 200, Colorado Springs, CO 80920

06 07 08 09 10 11 12 13 14 15   10 9 8 7 6 5 4 3 2 1

Edited by Between the Lines
Interior design by Tennille Paden
Cover design by Terry Dugan
Photography/illustrations by Robert Parham, Visions West Fine Art Photography

Library of Congress Cataloging-in-Publication Data

Lueders, Beth.
    Two days longer : discovering more of God as you wait for him / Beth Lueders.
        p. cm.
    Includes bibliographical references.
    ISBN 1-58229-490-9
    1. Spiritual life—Christianity. 2. Patience—Religious aspects—Christianity. I. Title.

BV4647.P3L84 2006
248.4—dc22

                                                                    2005055134

To Mom and Dad,

who modeled that good things do come to those who wait.

Contents

Contents

Acknowledgments

Soli Deo Gloria! Without the inspiration and direction of my Creator and the prayers and advice of my friends and colleagues, this book would not exist. I am truly honored by so many of you who continually believe in me. I wish I had the space here to thank each of you by name.

I am deeply grateful for the sustaining wisdom and laughter of my "fan club." You lighten my load and help me cherish what really matters in life. I owe plenty of chocolate and lattes to Angie Boyd, Terry Cornuke, Julie Cox, Karen DeLorenzo, Lisa Dorman, Diane Fritsch, Shelly Johnson, Debbie Krumland, Laura Lisle, Kathy Parham, Kristi Phipps, and Daria Wegner.

Ellen Alcala, Candace Andrews, the Bible Babes, Diana Bender, Carrie Brandt, Linda Brown, RoJean Clifton, Tejae Floyde, Scott and Ann Hewitt, Renee Hoobyar, Chris Kaupp, Teri Nott, Bill and Vickie Markham, Philis Moberly, Guy Moore, Ray and Jean Moore, Rob Parham, Carolyn Protic, Donna Stark, Joli Storm, Jeanine Talge, and Lila Tooker—your friendship and prayers settle me down when I tire of waiting.

Lee Hough, I appreciate your wise and gracious counsel. Philis Boultinghouse, Dawn Brandon, Tammy Bicket, and the excellent team at Howard Publishing, I thank you for your professional guidance.

Finally, a warm thanks to all of you reading this book. Trust me . . . waiting on God is always worth the wait.

Lingering by the River

Your Timely God

God longs to reveal himself, to fill us with himself.
Waiting on God gives him time in his own way
and divine power to come to us.

Andrew Murray

Jawad Amer Sayed crouched in the three-foot-wide chamber, resting his eye against a peephole barely the size of his finger. Peering through this miniscule window, Jawad could see only the inner courtyard of his farmhouse. But for a man holed up in a wall, any view of the outside world was better than staring at his dirt-and-mortar cell.

Most people considered Jawad long dead. He, at times, thought the same. Only his mother, young brother, two sisters, and an aunt knew what had happened to Jawad in their Iraqi community one hundred miles southeast of Baghdad.

As a Shiite Muslim follower of the al-Dawa Party, Jawad risked imprisonment and death for his beliefs. For decades the al-Dawa Party battled the barbarous Iraqi dictator Saddam Hussein. Saddam's bloodthirsty secret police recorded in chilling detail the personal profiles, pictures, and entire history of thousands of Dawa Party members.

These files were stored in an underground complex below the headquarters of the Special Security Organization, ruled by Qusay, Saddam's most trusted son. One room alone in this cavernous vault, the size of two football fields, contained the files for one million critics of the tyrannical regime.

Jawad suspected his file was growing among this massive collection. "Fortunate" insurgents were only burned with cigarettes or raped. Reportedly millions were gruesomely tortured; at least a million Iraqis were killed. In 1981 Hussein's secret police arrested and executed two of Jawad's friends. Terrified that he would be next, Jawad resorted to drastic measures.

Instead of going into exile like many Dawa members, Jawad condemned himself to solitary confinement in his home—inside a false wall he built between two rooms. The day he saw his friends' names on the execution list, the twenty-seven-year-old Iraqi retreated to his farmhouse and built the seven-foot-long cubbyhole overnight.

Jawad dug a well at one end of the compartment and placed a toilet at the other end. He piled the excavated dirt to shape a terraced living area and built a dirt platform for sitting in the middle of the three-foot-wide chamber. He could stand and bathe in the lowest point of the walled cell. A vent to the roof let in fresh air, and a pipe drained water outside.

Jawad crawled into his narrow cell through a trap door hidden under a bed. His mother agreed to deliver fruit and vegetables through this opening. The Shiite Muslim huddled inside his dank hiding place and waited.

He waited for the secret police to lose the scent of his trail. He waited for the Dawas and other Islamic political parties to rally and deliver their nation from Saddam's death grip.

ONLY HIS MOTHER, YOUNG BROTHER, TWO SISTERS, AND AN AUNT KNEW WHAT HAD HAPPENED TO JAWAD ONE HUNDRED MILES SOUTHEAST OF BAGHDAD.

Jawad waited almost his entire adult life—twenty-two years—inside the confines of a camouflaged wall. He endured two decades and two years isolated from humanity.

On April 10, 2003, the day after Saddam Hussein fell from power, Jawad Amer Sayed emerged from his homemade crypt. He had only briefly left the cramped chamber twice in all those years to make repairs. During his extreme isolation, all of Jawad's teeth fell out. He stored them in a matchbox. Once taller than his five-foot-eight neighbor, Jawad now stands barely as high as his friend's nose.

A few weeks into his newfound freedom, with visitors and admirers at his side, the forty-nine-year-old Jawad talked of finding work and, maybe, a wife. "I enjoy sleeping outside now," he said. "Looking at the stars. But sometimes I like to go into the wall. It is my second home."

In reflecting on his twenty-two years of waiting in self-imposed solitary confinement, Jawad explained, "Most of the time, it was very, very quiet. I think only death could be so quiet."[1]

I can't imagine waiting for twenty-two years, in hibernation, away from communication with others, away from everyday conveniences. I struggle sometimes to wait twenty-two seconds, let alone twenty-two hours . . . twenty-two days . . . twenty-two weeks.

Horrific fear and desperation bulldozed Jawad. The choice was death or waiting. Jawad chose to wait. Most of us will never face such an extreme period of waiting alone. Yet when we're waiting on the God of the universe, even a few seconds can seem like an eternity.

Such was the case for a family that lived some 450 miles west of Jawad in the hillside settlement of Bethany. In their village, southeast of Jerusalem, two sisters, Mary and Martha, anguished at the bedside of their ill brother, Lazarus. The Bible's only recording of this account, John 11, does not identify Lazarus's sickness. But Lazarus's weakened condition was grave enough for the family to summon their dear friend Jesus.

The sisters sent a succinct plea to the Messiah: "Lord, the one you love is sick" (John 11:3).

Jesus was camping with his disciples along the Jordan River, about fifteen miles away from Lazarus's home. Even walking in the desert heat, with some hills to climb, Jesus could have hurried and reached Bethany within a day. But he chose another path. With his good buddy near death, Jesus decided to just hang out. Linger a while by the river.

John 11:6 informs us: "He then stayed two days longer in the place where He was" (NASB). Two days longer. What was the loving Messiah thinking! How could the Son of God turn his back on his much-loved comrade and just dawdle by the river? Was he having so much fun skipping rocks on the Jordan that he couldn't tear himself away?

Maybe that's what you're thinking. Or perhaps you're wondering when this loving God will show up in your time of need. Maybe you're enduring your own season of delay—two days . . . two months . . . two years . . . two decades.

The long-awaited spouse. The hoped-for baby. The agonizing medical unknowns. The anxious pacing over a rebellious teen. The promised money that never comes.

Ever tire of holding your breath and twiddling your thumbs, expecting life to turn around? Ever think of God more as the Dillydallying Divine than the Punctual Providence?

I'm sure this crossed Mary's and Martha's minds as they huddled around the failing Lazarus. Surely doubts surfaced about this Jesus who drifted around Palestine healing people he didn't even know but who now refused to aid one of his cherished friends.

When it comes to questioning God, I admit I'm somewhat of an aficionado. But a number of years ago I met someone who altered my habit of interrogating God. Alice transformed how I see and believe in the God who at times makes us all wait.

———————————

Stooped over from years of arduous farmwork and caring for her younger sister, Alice shuffles across her tiny living room. Joining me on the sagging couch, this eighty-something widow slides a glass of iced tea my way and wipes her crinkled brow with an embroidered white handkerchief. Gingerly she tucks the dainty cloth inside the sleeve of her cotton dress and offers me a homemade oatmeal cookie. Sister Elsie scoots her creaky rocker near us. Elsie smiles and nods, nods and smiles—the simple language of an elderly woman slowed by a childhood case of scarlet fever.

Struggling to survive in a paint-peeled farmhouse amid steamy cornfields and tall, spindly prairie grasses, these two sisters give me more than their sacrificial dollars for my Christian mission work. Alice and Elsie shower me with prayer and wise advice.

With arthritis-gnarled fingers, Alice opens her dog-eared Bible on the wobbly coffee table. She turns a few pages and pauses to peer at me over her thin, wire-framed glasses. "Dear, do you know the two most powerful words in all-l-l the Bible?" Alice asks in her quivery, soft voice.

I sip my iced tea, trying to recall key two-word combinations in God's Word. *Almighty God, Jesus Christ, eternal life,* and others come to mind, but I finally just shrug. "The two most powerful words? Uh . . . I'm not sure, Alice."

"But God!" Alice firmly volunteers with her right index finger shaking right at me. "But God! You know why? Because when situations look their worst and we are weary from waiting, God steps in and proves that he is all-powerful, loving, and wise. Remember the story of Joseph and how his brothers left him for dead? But God spared his life and blessed him with prosperity in Pharaoh's court. Here, honey, read out loud Joseph's words to his brothers from Genesis 45:8 and 50:20."

> HE MAY SEEM LIKE AN ELEVENTH-HOUR GOD, BUT OUR JEHOVAH JIREH IS NEVER LATE WITH HIS ANSWERS.

Eagerly I read from Alice's Bible: "Now, therefore, it was not you who sent me here, *but God*; and He has made me a father to Pharaoh and lord of all his household and ruler over all the land of Egypt. . . . As for you, you meant evil against me, *but God* meant it for good in order to bring about this present result, to preserve many people alive" (NASB, emphasis added).

That summer afternoon in a back-roads Nebraska farmhouse, I

leaned into every word Alice shared about the Bible's two most powerful words. Now, some fifteen years later, as my wise friend rejoices in her heavenly mansion, I cherish her sage advice. With two brief words, this seasoned saint reformed my view of a majestic God who always intervenes at just the right moment. He may seem like an eleventh-hour God, but our Jehovah Jireh is never late with his answers.

God often deals in cliff-hangers and last-minute answers. Have you ever noticed that some of the most white-knuckled, edge-of-your-seat moments in world history are recorded in the Bible? We see a classic God-style suspense drama in the blockbuster movies *The Ten Commandments* and *The Prince of Egypt*. In these award-winning films we come face-to-face with millions of exasperated people waiting on their Creator. For decades the enslaved Israelites literally sweat it out, expecting God to set them free. But once out of bondage, the people were forced to cool their heels and wait again.

Reading the original account in Exodus 12–14, we find the infuriated Egyptian pharaoh and his army's chariots barreling down on the Israelite refugees like Navy SEALs pursuing unarmed families fleeing for their lives. Perhaps what really got Pharaoh's goat . . . or camel . . . is the fact that these freed captives are led by Moses, royal insider turned rebel with a cause.

Notice how the on-the-run Israelites respond when they see the Egyptian dictator and his military in hot pursuit. Terrified, they cry out to God. Next, they interrogate Moses: "Was it because there were no graves in Egypt that you brought us to the desert to die? What have you done to us by bringing us out of Egypt? Didn't we say to you in Egypt, 'Leave us alone; let us serve the Egyptians'? It would have been better for us to serve the Egyptians than to die in the desert!" (Exodus 14:11–12).

The people's fierce criticism of Moses is really directed at God. "God, are you stupid? Aren't there enough graves where we just came from? Do you need to fill cemeteries in this desert with our bodies? Didn't you hear us when we said, 'Leave us alone. We'd rather be slaves than die in this parched wasteland?' We've waited for you long enough!"

How often that sounds like me and, I'm guessing, even you at times. But just when it looks like a major mutiny is brewing against Moses, this Exodus chronicle crescendos with a "but God" intervention. Jehovah listens to his children's pleas and directs Moses to raise his staff over the Red Sea. A path of dry land forms, and the people escape just before the colossal walls of water collapse on their enemies.

Often in pressing challenges we, like the ancient Israelites, demand that God part the waters for us *now*! We employ the "but God" phrase a little differently—a common response of our faint and droopy spirits. When we stumble on disappointment or nearly suffocate in a quagmire of red tape, we rant for God to answer us immediately. When we can't control life, God is often the first one we accuse. But God, how could you? But God, why me, why us, why now? But God, if you really care, where are you?

Though we may demand that life treat us fairly, it will never completely bend to our expectations or keep to our timetable. Day-to-day waiting is tough, no matter who we are or where we live. For some, waiting means accepting more delays in loved ones' coming home; for others it means filling out yet another job application or holding out hope that researchers will find a cure.

At some point we are all banished to the prison of postponement. Since the day Adam and Eve snacked on the forbidden fruit, humanity has anguished over the loss of an idyllic world with no delays. No matter how hard we try, we can never elude the necessity to wait on God.

In my travels to seventeen countries, I've hurled a number of "but God" pleas toward heaven as I've encountered holdups in my life and in the lives of countless others. My mind wanders to the radiation-poisoned children of Chernobyl, whom I met during a humanitarian-relief trip. But God . . . couldn't you speed up their recovery?

I think of the Manila prostitutes I interviewed, who night after night line darkened alleys as attractive prey for lustful johns. But God . . . can't you hurry up and provide other work for these young women?

Perhaps you, like me, have questioned God's hearing and eyesight: But God, are you deaf to my cries? Can't you see what I'm facing?

When glandular skin cancer clawed its way into my mother's life, I shook my clenched fist at the Master Physician. How could you let the surgeons irreparably scar her face? How could you leave her walking with an unsteady shuffle? I railed against the Almighty later when a stroke stole her life at age seventy.

As I write this, grief gnaws at my heart and I must pause. But God, why did you let her suffer so long? But God, in her coma did she really hear our last good-byes? Intense questions. No simple answers.

You've undoubtedly posed your own "but God" questions as you or those you love have waited and watched for God, who sometimes seems stuck in the clog of rush-hour traffic on his way to rescue his people.

Yet while toe-tapping and pleading with God to pick up his pace, we must not forget the *but* in the "but God" equation. *But* means "on the contrary," "on the other hand." We may feel that God is pokey and doesn't care about us. But—*on the contrary*—God loves us deeply and is intimately "familiar with all [our] ways" (Psalm 139:3). *On the contrary*, God hears our cries and understands our pain. *On the contrary*, God intends good in our lives.

In John 11 we find that Jesus let Lazarus die. But—*on the other hand*—Jesus allowed Lazarus to live again. Why did Jesus drag his sandals two days longer in the Judean wilderness? He could have done what Mary and Martha thought was the best thing; but, *on the other hand*, he had a superior plan, "that the Son of God may be glorified" (John 11:4 NKJV).

Before Jesus headed to Bethany, he explained to his disciples, "You're about to be given new grounds for believing" (John 11:15 MSG). Jesus tarried so he could raise Lazarus from the dead and show the world—even you and me—new grounds for believing who he really is.

Through waiting, God wants to open our nearsighted eyes to the vivid depths of his immense character. He invites us to nestle into the assurance that he is loving, faithful, all-powerful, and trustworthy. On the other hand, he wants us to consider him punctual and not a latecomer. He wants us to delight in Jesus-on-the-spot and not Jesus-come-lately.

> THE QUESTION IS, ARE WE WILLING TO WAIT FOR GOD TO SHOW UP, EVEN IF IT APPEARS THAT HE'S LOITERING BY THE RIVERSIDE?

The question is, are we willing to wait for God to show up, even if it appears that he's loitering by the riverside?

Joseph waited, languishing in a dank prison cell. Moses waited even as Pharaoh's fierce armies thundered closer. Jesus waited on a bloody cross while his friends and even his own father, it seemed, abandoned him. In anticipating that God would come through, these men of faith kept their eyes on their Sustainer and not on their situations. Even if they never saw God show up in the way they hoped, they refused to buckle or bend to defeat and despair.

You may be at this crucial point yourself. How do you keep holding out hope in God when you feel certain he's detained in some celestial gridlock? In waiting you may not see the final outcome of your prayers and persistence, but deep within the caverns of your soul, God is gently tapping.

Through life's delays, God is at work—often behind the scenes—to draw us into a richer experience of knowing him more intimately. While we pace and sweat it out, nervous and impatient for God to intervene, he longs for us to rest in his love, his compassion, and his peace. The reward of waiting on God does not come in circumstances and timing that satisfy our expectations; the reward comes in God himself.

If God can reunite Joseph with his brothers, divide the sea for Moses, and resurrect Jesus from the dead, then surely he can intervene in any situation we encounter. He can—but he may not respond on our timetable. God's perspective of time encompasses all of eternity, while our focus is primarily on the here and now.

But we can rest easy as we wait. God will always weave together good from our dangling shreds of disappointment and weariness—even if, this side of heaven, we can't see the lustrous beauty of the tapestry he's weaving. God will always step away from the river, even if we must wait . . . and sometimes wait longer than we'd like.

Seeing Is Believing

Your All-Seeing God

When it is dark enough, men see the stars.

Ralph Waldo Emerson

Tuesday morning, September 11, 2001, Lt. Col. Brian Birdwell sits stunned in his boss's office, watching televised images of a second hijacked airplane slamming into New York City's World Trade Center. The army officer has no idea that minutes later madmen will ram a Boeing 757 into the Pentagon, just three windows away from his office.

At 9:40 a.m. Brian steps out of the men's room and heads down the hallway back to his desk. Suddenly a thunderous explosion hurls him to the floor. A churning fireball and thick, acrid smoke engulf the dazed officer. His body is on fire. Brian can't get to his feet. He agonizes that he will never again see his wife, Mel, and his twelve-year-old son, Matthew. Brian screams, "Jesus, I'm coming to see you!" The officer closes his eyes and waits for death to free him from the immense pain.

Around the globe millions of people rally around television sets in homes, offices, restaurants, airports, stores, anywhere they can catch a glimpse of the unfolding chaos in America. The world watches and waits.

In their Virginia home, not far from the smoldering Pentagon, Mel Birdwell and her son sit mesmerized, watching ghastly footage of monstrous flames and smoke billow from the crumbling Pentagon. "I knew right away Brian's office could not have survived that impact," Mel says, recalling those agonizing moments in front of their television.

Mom and son tearfully pray together for Brian, hoping that he was out of his office at the time of the crash. Matthew then hollers, punches a wall, and storms outside for a walk. Mel calls a friend to come over and be with her. The waiting is just beginning.

Collapsed on the floor amid debris, Brian squints into the smoky darkness. He prays, asking God to take care of Mel and Matthew. The Gulf War veteran can no longer feel the flames scorching his body. He expects his life to end any second.

But then come the drops of water. Plop, plunk . . . plop, plunk . . . plop, plunk. In his struggle to escape the inferno, Brian had fallen under an overhead fire sprinkler. The cooling relief trickles over his charred wounds. Staying flat on the floor to avoid the choking smoke above him, Brian peers down the hallway. Gaining a sense of direction, the severely wounded officer struggles to his feet, hunching over from the immense pain. He stumbles along for a few yards before collapsing at the feet of a fellow officer looking for survivors. Pentagon workers carry Brian to safety outside.

"I saw at least four other people being treated at the triage site," Brian recalls later. "But I was the first one taken away, so that told me I was in pretty bad shape." Most of the 189 dead never even made it to triage.

Mel paces and prays at home for an hour and a half before finally receiving a phone call saying her husband is alive. A friend stays with Matthew while a neighbor drives Mel to the Georgetown hospital, where Brian was admitted. But chaos and blocked roads hold traffic to a crawl.

"It seemed like it took an eternity to get to the hospital," Mel recounts. "As we drove, fear and panic flooded my mind. I called the hospital several times to be sure nothing had changed."

When they find the Francis Scott Key Bridge closed, Mel bolts from the car and starts running across the 1.6-mile span. "About halfway across the bridge, I stopped and looked toward the Pentagon," Mel says. "Seeing the smoke just spewing out of it was the most horrific, overwhelming sight."

THE OFFICER CLOSES HIS EYES AND WAITS FOR DEATH TO FREE HIM FROM THE IMMENSE PAIN.

Mel runs frantically for a mile and half. Then she flags down a police officer, and he drives her the rest of the way to the hospital. Finally, after two torturous hours, a nerve-racked Mel rushes into the triage unit, where nurses update her about her husband's dire condition. Flames seared more than 60 percent of Brian's body—his hands, arms, face, ears, legs, and back. Nearly half of the burns were third degree, the rest second degree. Inhaled toxic smoke scorched the lining of his lungs. For days Brian hovers between life and death.

Gradually Brian begins breathing without a ventilator, just a few minutes at a time, to exercise his weakened lungs—baby steps for the once-fit soldier. A ravaging staff infection gnaws away at the remaining flesh on both arms. Brian endures excruciating chlorine-and-iodine baths in which nurses scrub away dangling layers of decayed skin. More than thirty surgeries are necessary to cleanse wounds, graft on fresh skin, and reconstruct his ears. The twelve weeks of in-patient hospital care are the longest of Brian's then forty years.

I first talked with Brian a few days after his release from the hospital. The Birdwells were gracious to grant me an interview for a 9/11 booklet about hope and courage. Even when those bleakest days were behind him, the Texas native still faced nearly a year of physical therapy to regain his strength and mobility. Yet the Pentagon hero did not focus on what he lost in the attack, but what he gained.

"My living through all this is one of God's many miracles," Brian said. "This testing by fire, so to speak, has strengthened our marriage and faith. My priorities of Mel, Matt, and the army have not changed; I've just learned to relish and appreciate these priorities more readily."

One of the main factors that kept the Birdwells clinging to hope was knowing that they trust in a God who sees everything. "There's nothing in life that hasn't either been sifted by the Lord or he's carrying you through. You can see the hand of the Lord in so many things from September 11 that just didn't happen because of chance, luck, or fate," Brian explained. "That includes the number of people who could have been killed that day to the towers collapsing straight down instead of crumbling over.

"That's also everything from my surviving the blast and the concussion and not being unconscious to the sprinkler system going off. It's also my being the one burn victim to make it to the Georgetown hospital, where doctors trained in burn treatment just happened to be on duty. You cannot look at September 11 and all the events that led to my survival and view them as random acts. Man does not view the events of September 11 in an omnipotent way like God does."

God saw the terrorist suicide assailants board American Airlines Flight 77 that September morning. God saw these mass murderers commandeer the Los Angeles–bound plane and veer it toward the Pentagon. God saw each individual at work in the corridors of the Pentagon building. God saw Brian drop to the floor under the sprinklers.

God saw Mel and Matthew agonizing at home. God saw the coworkers carry Brian to triage. God saw Mel running on that bridge. God saw every damaged skin cell on Brian's body.

God saw a family and a country draw together in a time of unprecedented personal and national tragedy. God saw every second of September 11, 2001, just as he sees every second of this day. Nothing escapes his notice—not even the circumstances in your life, whether monumental or mundane.

The ancient Hebrews called this all-seeing God *El Roi*. We are first introduced to this name for Jehovah halfway through the Bible's first book. In Genesis 16 we read of Sarai, a woman exasperated by a decade of waiting for a child. But infertility wasn't her only trouble. Sarai could have been the poster girl for Tammy Wynette's 1968 hit "Stand by Your Man."

Married to the Chaldean Abram, Sarai endures a plethora of

experiences and conditions that might have seemed like good reasons to run from her nomadic husband. Genesis chapters 12 and 13 detail Abram and Sarai's Canaan travel: arrive at Shechem, move on to the hills of Bethel, then mosey down to Negev. When famine hits, they journey west to Egypt. There Abram, in a cowardly act of self-preservation, abandons his beautiful wife to the arms of Pharaoh. While Abram passes Sarai off as his sister, he accumulates herds of livestock and several servants.

Abram betrays Sarai, but we don't read of her rebelling and telling Abram where to head his sheep. At that point it seems Sarai could croon, "Wait for Your Man."

The aging couple returns with their ever-increasing possessions to Negev and eventually settles in Hebron. There in the land of Canaan, God promises Abram vast lands for his many offspring. But what offspring? Abram has heard similar God-talk before (see Genesis 12:2). But that was ten years and thousands of dusty miles ago, and although lovely Sarai is aging gracefully, she is well beyond her childbearing years.

> HE'S THE SAME GOD WHO SEES US WAITING BY THE PHONE, WAITING THROUGH OUR TEARS, WAITING IN PRAYER.

For her part, Sarai is tired of holding her horses—er, camels. After a disappointing decade of waiting for God to open her womb, she decides to help God out. One day she blurts out to Abram, "Go, sleep with my maidservant; perhaps I can build a family through her" (Genesis 16:2). Sarai presents her Egyptian servant Hagar to Abram as a second wife. In Sarai's mind it seems that desperate times call for desperate measures. Oh, how I can relate to that reasoning!

When Hagar becomes pregnant with Abram's child, the maid despises her mistress. The tension between the women escalates, and Sarai blames the soon-to-be father for her feelings of jealousy and inadequacy. She rants at Abram, "You are responsible for the wrong I am suffering" (Genesis 16:5).

Abram deflects Sarai's wrath with, "Your servant is in your hands. . . . Do with her whatever you think best" (Genesis 16:6). So Sarai vents her built-up frustration on Hagar. No doubt dealing with her own fluctuating hormones, pregnant Hagar dumps her job and new husband and heads for the desert.

We next find Hagar resting at the spring along the road to Shur. The angel of the Lord approaches and tells the troubled Hagar to return to Sarai and Abram. The divine messenger directs the runaway maid to name her yet-unborn son Ishmael, which means "God hears." The angel reassures Hagar, "The LORD has heard of your misery" (Genesis 16:11).

Perhaps moved by the words of God's spokesperson, Hagar cries out to her Creator, "You are the God who sees me. . . . I have now seen the One who sees me" (Genesis 16:13). Hagar's Hebrew words for her all-seeing God are *El Roi*. Sitting in the desert sands, this parched mom-to-be is revived by El Roi, who sees her predicament and pain. The well where Hagar encounters God is then named Beer Lahai Roi, "the well of the living one who sees me."

The God who sees. The God who sees an army officer trapped in an inferno is the same God who sees a homeless pregnant woman slumped at a desert well. He's the same God who sees us waiting by the phone, waiting through our tears, waiting in prayer.

Gifted speaker and author Richard Foster has said, "One of the greatest expressions of love is simply to notice people and to pay attention to them."[1] That's what God does—he notices, he pays attention—even when we think he's blind and indifferent.

Yet do we really get it—that God sees *everything* in our lives? How often in my waiting I treat God as though he were severely visually impaired and needed corrective lenses.

But the longer I wait with him, the more I realize that God's eyesight is always better than 20/20. It's my eyes that need corrective help. What about you? Do you ever feel that God is blind to your needs, your desires, your hopes? Waiting can teach us to tug the bandages off our eyes and gaze upon the majesty of our God.

In the movie *At First Sight*, Val Kilmer plays Virgil Adamson, a blind masseur who lost his full sight to congenital cataracts at age three. Virgil falls in love with a client, Amy Benic, played by Mira Sorvino. Amy encourages Virgil to undergo experimental surgery to try to correct his damaged eyes. After surgery the prominent eye surgeon slowly peels the bandages from Virgil's eyes. The suspense is excruciating. First the left eye, then the right. A camera crew for the ophthalmology center is on hand to capture the dramatic unveiling.

The camera zooms in on Virgil's bruised eyes. He squints and grimaces. Slowly his reddish-purple eyelids open. His eyelids strain against the incoming light. Blurred, grayish shadows swim across Virgil's field of vision. The people in the room appear as looming, floating images.

"Can you see Amy?" the surgeon asks eagerly.

"I'm over here, Virgil," Amy gently explains.

"I don't know," Virgil mumbles as he aims his blurry eyes toward his girlfriend's reassuring voice.

Panic grips Virgil. "This isn't right! Something is wrong," Virgil stammers as he repeatedly squeezes his eyes shut, then opens them. "This can't be seeing!"

A few scenes later we find Virgil and Amy in the office of a noted visual therapist, Dr. Webster. They seek Dr. Webster's counsel on how to eliminate Virgil's visual distortion and improve his ability to recognize new images. After thirtysome years of functioning in a dark, sightless world, Virgil is unable to identify and process many shapes, colors, and dimensions.

"There's only been twenty cases of this in the last two hundred years," Dr. Webster says after a brief evaluation of Virgil. "Basically your eyes work, but your brain hasn't learned to process the information. You are mentally blind."

> OUR EYES WORK, BUT OUR BRAINS AND HEARTS HAVE NOT LEARNED TO PROCESS WHAT WE SEE ABOUT GOD. WE'RE SPIRITUALLY BLIND.

Sometimes we're just like Virgil Adamson. Our eyes work, but our brains and hearts have not learned to process what we see about God. We're spiritually blind. We can read scores of Bible passages and inspirational books that declare, like Hagar, "You are the God who sees me. I have now seen the One who sees me." But our impatience in waiting and our urge to rearrange our lives as we see fit cloud our perception of the all-seeing God.

I remember one summer when my eyes clouded over with national pride and superiority. During a three-week mission trip to five overseas countries, I began to focus on my familiar world of comfort, convenience, and choice back home.

One day as I rode the Metro, Moscow's high-speed subway, I found myself temporarily cocooned with hundreds of strangers. On a normal

21

weekday some eight million people pack into Metro cars at 165 stations. The Metro is like a crammed ballroom of somber travelers, all swaying and tilting to the cadence of the streaking train. Shuffle. Lean. Shuffle. Lean. Few people speak. No one smiles.

Nonchalantly shifting my eyes from passenger to passenger, I noticed several Muscovites sheepishly glancing at my feet—a Westerner's shoes scream of democracy and dollars. Typically, Russians' shoes are plastic, worn, dirtied, simple. Many own only one pair. No pumps, heels, or loafers to match every outfit. No shoe polish.

Jostling out of the underground tunnel with the hordes of stone-faced passengers, I nearly stumbled over a hunchbacked babushka sweeping the sidewalk with her tiny twig broom. Suddenly it was as if crusty scales flaked off of my eyes. My myopia—focusing on my schedule, my priorities, my needs—began to lift. For one brief moment the Master Ophthalmologist adjusted my eyesight so I could see what really matters in this world—God and the diverse people he created.

I began to comprehend that the same God who sees a babushka walk in shabby shoes day after day in slushy snow, over lumpy fields, through junk-strewn alleys is the same God who sees me walk in polished boots across immaculately manicured lawns and luxuriously thick carpet. What if God closed his eyes to the scuffed-shoed or babushkas of the world? What if he closed his eyes to me or to you?

In anxious times of waiting, I find tremendous hope and strength in fixing my eyes on who God really is—the El Roi. In the midst of Job's listless suffering and grief, he declared that God "views the ends of the earth and sees everything under the heavens" (Job 28:24). A little later, in Job 34:21, the weary yet hope-filled Job asserted: "His eyes are on the ways of men; he sees their every step."

God sees our every step, whether we wear shabby shoes or high-gloss boots, or we go barefoot. King David said, "From heaven the

LORD looks down and sees all mankind; from his dwelling place he watches all who live on earth—he who forms the hearts of all, who considers everything they do" (Psalm 33:13–15).

God sees; God watches. God waits with us. "Nothing in all creation is hidden from God's sight. Everything is uncovered and laid bare before the eyes of him to whom we must give account" (Hebrews 4:13). As we wait for our all-seeing God, our good deeds, our moral mishaps, our faintness of heart are laid bare before him. Nothing is farther than God's eyes can see. Not even death.

Lazarus died. Yet even though the Son of God tarried by the Jordan, Lazarus's last breath did not escape Jesus's notice. No relative called the Messiah on his cell phone to inform him of his close comrade's death. No obituary e-mail zipped out to update Jesus along the riverside.

The God who sees knew the exact second when Lazarus passed from this life. He then informed his disciples that they would be heading back to Judea because "Lazarus is dead" (John 11:14). From afar Jesus "saw" his dear friend die, and he saw the right time to join the mourners. This Jesus with perfect vision is the same God who preached to the crowds, "Blessed are your eyes because they see" (Matthew 13:16).

Are our eyes open and expectant to see God work on our behalf? A Japanese proverb wisely says, "Daylight will peep through a very small hole."[2] Waiting for answers, for a sign of hope, is like waiting in the dark for a sliver of daylight. But since when is our all-seeing God confined to a very small hole?

———————

Many fearless climbers who've set foot on Mount Everest understand the waiting for a sliver of daylight to peek through dense clouds and blustering snow. Towering in the Himalayas along the Nepal-Tibet border, the world's highest peak looms at 29,035 feet.

In 1953 Edmund Hillary and Tenzing Norgay were the first two people to ascend Everest. Since that historic climb, roughly two thousand men and women from more than sixty nations have tackled the summit. Nearly two hundred others have died trying. In the early morning hours of May 25, 2001, one man rewrote history on Mount Everest.

Erik Weihenmayer of Denver, Colorado, became the first blind person to conquer the revered mountain. A few days after Erik stood on the famous peak, the world-class athlete rested at the base of Everest and talked by telephone with CNN anchor Carol Lin. Having lost his sight at age thirteen, Erik redefined for the whole world what it means to be blind.

In the CNN interview Erik quickly gave credit to his twenty-plus Everest teammates and his generous sponsors, including the National Federation of the Blind. When Carol asked the adventure climber what he relied on to get to the summit, Erik eagerly described what helped him "see" over steep terrain, riddled with icefalls and massive crevasses.

"I follow somebody who climbs in front of you with a bell. And they jingle a bell from their ice ax or from their ski pole or from whatever is there. They'll just hold it. And I'll listen to them, and they'll call out directions," Erik explained. "They'll say, 'big drop off' or 'steep climb' . . . and sometimes you're crossing these very narrow snow bridges. So they tell me exactly where to step."[3]

Sometimes, as we wait, our perceptions get distorted and we can't see God. We lose sight of our path and slip off into harrowing crevasses of anger, despair, and apathy. But somehow, just when we think we're abandoned on the dark side of a desolate mountain, God jingles a little bell. Calmly he reassures us, "It's OK. I'm over here. Keep stepping straight ahead. We're going to make it together. It won't be much longer."

I love how the prophet Isaiah describes our all-seeing God guiding us up life's impossible mountains: "Whether you turn to the right or to the left, your ears will hear a voice behind you, saying, 'This is the way; walk in it'" (Isaiah 30:21).

In your season of waiting, can you hear God jingling a bell tuned just for you? Lean in; listen closely. Keep placing one foot in front of the other. In time you'll be able to respond as Job did after his ordeal of suffering and waiting: "My ears had heard of you but now my eyes have seen you" (Job 42:5).

CHAPTER THREE

When God Stops
Your Compassionate God

Man may dismiss compassion from his heart,
but God never will.

William Cowper

Coolidge Winesett wails until his voice fades to a raspy whisper. When the floor of his rural Virginia outhouse collapses and the earth below swallows him whole, the seventy-five-year-old finds himself trapped alive.

From the outhouse pit, Coolidge hollers at a neighbor hammering nails: "Randy, Randy, Randy, Randy . . ." He yells to a neighbor mowing a lawn: "Gary, Gary, Gary, Gary . . ." After an hour of shouting for help, the elderly man grows silent and closes his eyes.

Wedged against a muddy wall fifteen feet down, Coolidge sits suspended a few feet above the sewage. The stench nearly strangles him. He heaves shallow breaths. If help doesn't come soon, Coolidge will wish that death will.

Flies crawl on him, and a rat stares him in the eyes. A tiny black snake slithers across his muddied forehead. From Saturday afternoon until the following Tuesday afternoon, Coolidge lingers in the reeking pit. He hallucinates. He prays.

> WEDGED AGAINST A MUDDY WALL FIFTEEN FEET DOWN, COOLIDGE SITS SUSPENDED A FEW FEET ABOVE THE SEWAGE.

For nearly four days no one hears Coolidge's cries from the caved-in latrine. But in Ivanhoe, Virginia, with a population of five hundred, it's hard to go missing for long. Finally, on Tuesday, postal carrier Jimmy Jackson suspects something is amiss and wanders behind the house. He calls out to the former high-school janitor and hears a faint "whooo" coming from the collapsed privy.

Later, from his hospital bed, the recovering Coolidge describes his fight for survival. "The nights were the longest. . . . The nights would get so quiet. Couldn't hear nobody 'round," Coolidge recalled. "No chance of help. I thought for sure I was a goner."

Relieved that he had found the almost-buried-alive Coolidge, Jimmy said, "People joke about it—what with it being an outhouse and all—but that poor ol' man almost died. Thank God he hung on."[11]

Hanging on when we've been thrown into a pit, or feel like we have, is no easy feat. Coolidge Winesett could probably relate to the words of the psalmist: "He lifted me out of the slimy pit, out of the mud and mire; he set my feet on a rock and gave me a firm place to stand" (Psalm 40:2).

<hr>

We all need a firm place to stand when we're waiting on God. Whether we're trapped in a rank outhouse pit or trapped in the mire of unmet expectations and delayed plans, we need the steady hand of God, "who redeems your life from the pit and crowns you with love and compassion" (Psalm 103:4).

I found this particularly true for some Albanians I met during the thick-aired summer of 1993. I spent a week in Tirana, the capital of this formerly Communist country, helping introduce Albanian educators to classroom ethics.

Tirana, like hot-pepper ice cream, is a flavorful concoction of contrasts. It is an obscure world of children and elderly people, urban decay and country flowers, government sophisticates and scraggly beggars.

Day after day, along Tirana's uneven cobblestone streets, I walked past lean, dark-haired men nonchalantly passing their days flinging pebbles at scrawny dogs and napping on the steamy brick sidewalks.

Albania's national unemployment rate was horrific, so many of these college-educated unemployables squandered away afternoons sharing stories and imported cigarettes with their buddies. Some younger men proudly passed around faded photos of brothers and friends who had fled to Italy or Greece to find work and freedom. The mailed-home money from refugee loved ones kept many malnourished Albanians out of early graves.

Centuries of bloody purges, repression, and dictatorial leaders had devoured the hope and will of the Albanian people. Closer ties with Communist Russia and China after World War II led to the isolation of this Balkan country from the rest of the world. No televisions. No radios. No blue jeans. Speaking of God meant risking imprisonment.

Political freedom whispered its way across this poorest European country in the early 1990s. But the prolonged wait had already shoved many people into the pit of despondency.

Some desperate Albanians resorted to horrible acts of maiming their children and forcing them to beg on the streets. A child missing a hand or foot elicits more attention and thus more money. Other parents drugged their toddlers into a comatose state, sprawled them on squalid, tattered blankets along sidewalks, and hoped for a few crumpled bills or battered coins to drop their way.

I crossed paths with these disfigured and doped children almost every day. When I did, I squirmed with pity and anger. Why couldn't their parents just wait for the economy to pick up instead of taking such drastic measures? Why couldn't they wait for help?

Just when I pondered about these defenseless children, three or four of Tirana's healthier little ones would surround me, patting my back and extending their dirt-crusted hands and arms. Pointing to my purse, they'd sputter in broken English, "Dolla, madam, dolla, please."

I dared not look these solemn children in the eyes. Their heart-rending pleas for relief from suffering bore a haunting resemblance to the more articulate question I heard from adults throughout my stay in Albania: "Why has God allowed our country to suffer for so long?"

At heart all people everywhere wrestle with the same question: Why so long, God? And our sighs are similar to those of ancient people like King David, who lamented, "My soul is in anguish. How long, O

LORD, how long?" (Psalm 6:3). "How long, O LORD? Will you forget me forever? How long will you hide your face from me? How long must I wrestle with my thoughts and every day have sorrow in my heart? How long will my enemy triumph over me?" (Psalm 13:1–2). "How long must your servant wait?" (Psalm 119:84).

When I read the Bible's accounts of God's people snared in continuous wait mode, I find that we humans are not the only ones who ask, "How long?" Perhaps it's only fair that the Creator tosses the wearisome question back at his creations.

In the Old Testament we find the nation of Israel stunned by the fainthearted report of ten undercover agents who spied out the land of Canaan. After fleeing Egypt, Moses and the Israelites traipse around in the barren desert waiting for the day they would settle in the lush Promised Land. Day after day they trudge across sunbaked soil and live on manna wafers, only to find that their long-awaited paradise on earth is inhabited by giants (Numbers 13:32).

Disillusioned and disgruntled that God has led them astray, making them rough it as desert nomads, the Israelites rail and wail against the Almighty. They verbally assault their expedition leaders, Moses and Aaron, and cry for a new chief who will take them back to Egypt.

Just as the infuriated people threaten to stone Moses and his leadership team, God interrupts. He inquires of Moses: "How long will these people treat me with contempt? How long will they refuse to believe in me, in spite of all the miraculous signs I have performed among them?" (Numbers 14:11).

Touché! Fed up with waiting for his children to stop their whining, God jabs back with his own "how long?" retort. We find God again asking the infamous question of his wayward people during the tumultuous days of the prophets Jeremiah and Hosea.

"How long will you be unclean?" (Jeremiah 13:27). "How long will you wander, O unfaithful daughter?" (Jeremiah 31:22) "How long will they be incapable of purity?" (Hosea 8:5).

Even patient Jesus resorted to the "how long?" question when people failed to see that he was truly God. "'O unbelieving and perverse generation,' Jesus replied, 'how long shall I stay with you? How long shall I put up with you?'" (Matthew 17:17).

Many a day I find myself wondering if God stopped listening years ago to my cries of "how long?" Sometimes I feel like the impoverished Albanian kids begging for an end to my waiting. "Today . . . God . . . today . . . please." Other times I bear a striking resemblance to the Israelites in my wandering and whining as I wait.

How long do I have to wait to get married? (The plan was to wed right after college, but graduation was more than twenty years ago.) How long before my chronic neck and back pain subsides? (I haven't had a pain-free day since my first car accident in 1985.) How long before I breathe easier financially? (It's getting old every month trying to keep my business afloat.)

Waiting for relief from any situation causes us to confront the God we thought we knew. Does he really care? Where is his compassion? The dungeon of delay has its way of evoking gut-wrenching honesty with God and revealing our true perceptions of him. Is he on my side or not? Does he have a tender side, or is he just some power maniac?

How long . . . how long . . . how long? How long are we willing to wait for God? How long will God put up with us as we drum our fingers and grumble about his making us wait? Waiting involves both God and us.

In his classic book *Waiting on God*, South African theologian Andrew Murray described the sacred dance of waiting that occurs between man and his Maker:

We must not only think of our waiting upon God, but also of what is more wonderful still, of God's waiting upon us. The vision of him waiting on us, will give new impulse and inspiration to our waiting upon him. It will give an unspeakable confidence that our waiting cannot be in vain. . . . He waits with all the longings of a father's heart. He waits that he may be gracious unto you. . . . Yes, it is blessed when a waiting soul and a waiting God meet each other.[2]

What comfort to know that God is gently waiting for us with the "longings of a father's heart." What an encouragement to know that our souls are destined to meet his soul through the steps of waiting. What an honor to brush against the soul of God as we wait for him.

> THE DUNGEON OF DELAY HAS ITS WAY OF EVOKING GUT-WRENCHING HONESTY WITH GOD AND REVEALING OUR TRUE PERCEPTIONS OF HIM.

The poet and prophet Isaiah wrote: "The LORD longs to be gracious to you; he rises to show you compassion. . . . Blessed are all who wait for him!" (Isaiah 30:18). This gifted Jewish orator patiently preached to an obstinate crowd for about sixty years. Throughout the reign of at least four kings, Isaiah daily lived a life of holdups. Refined in the crucible of waiting, Isaiah urges us even today to look to God, especially when life stonewalls us.

At times, exhausted by waiting, we may feel like destitute children pleading for spare change; but God welcomes our pats on his arm, our tugs of his robe, our spurts of broken speech. "Today . . . God . . . today . . . please."

Why does God welcome our incessant patting, tugging, and

pleading? Because as Isaiah pointed out, the God who waits alongside us longs to shower us with compassion.

The story of a man who lived two thousand years ago draws us face-to-face with the God who is "full of compassion" (James 5:11).

Dependent on the generosity of others, the blind pauper Bartimaeus sits along the road on the outskirts of Jericho. At about eight hundred feet below sea level, hot and tropical Jericho (of Bible times and today) is situated lower than any other city on earth. The sweltering heat surely adds to Bartimaeus's challenge of waiting for handouts.

Although Bartimaeus can't see the camels, carts, and travelers kicking up the dirt on him that day, he must be feeling the grit caking onto his sun-weathered face. Suddenly a throng of people pour past him. No doubt the air thickens with dust and debris, and likely few in the rambunctious crowd can hear Bartimaeus inquire about the cause for the commotion. But some tell him that Jesus of Nazareth is approaching.

Surely Bartimaeus has heard about this healer who had been baptized three years earlier in the Jordan River not far from Jericho. Perhaps Bartimaeus has heard about Jesus's battle with Satan in the desolate Judean wilderness south of the city. Most likely Bartimaeus is acquainted with the centuries-old stories of Rahab's home in Jericho and Jehovah's display of power and miraculous works in this "city of palms."

We pick up the scene with Bartimaeus in Luke 18:38–39 where he calls out for Jesus, Son of David, to have mercy on him. Those leading the way rebuke Bartimaeus and urge him to be quiet, but he shouts all the more, 'Son of David, have mercy on me!'"

Bartimaeus, long scarred by the limitations of his blindness, calls out to Jesus. The sightless beggar doesn't utter a couple of words and then collapse into silence. This needy man SHOUTS. And I love the way Bartimaeus responds when the people try to silence him: "He shouted *all the more*" (emphasis added).

When we're caught in the clutches of waiting, and we're desperate for God's answers, it's natural to raise our voices asking for his help. It's natural to ignore other people's advice and appeal directly to the King. It's natural to shout all the more when we fear we won't be heard.

Just when we feel like a scrawny child or a blind man begging for a few scraps of relief, something incredible occurs. Verse 40 reveals this magnificent phenomenon in two simple words: "Jesus stopped."

Whoa! The on-a-mission God of the universe stops for a sightless stranger, a man many considered a vile vagabond, a blind bum, a pathetic panhandler. Amid the frenzy, God puts the world on hold and turns to his ailing child Bartimaeus. Mark 10:49 tells us that Jesus stops and directs his disciples and the multitude of followers, "Call him."

Not only does Jesus halt the entire procession for this roadside drifter, he then invites Bartimaeus to come to him. Mark explains that Bartimaeus immediately tosses aside his cloak and jumps up to greet the Messiah. Can you blame him? Waiting years and years for even a glimpse of faint sunlight, Bartimaeus seems to sense that the Light of the world is his only hope, both physically and spiritually.

How do you perceive this God who paused along a bustling roadway centuries ago? Do you believe he will pause for you today? I do because of one character quality in particular: compassion. But don't take my word for it; take God's.

Psalm 116:5 declares: "The LORD is gracious and righteous; our God is full of compassion." Psalm 145:8–9 reminds us: "The LORD is gracious and compassionate, slow to anger and rich in love. The LORD is good to all; he has compassion on all he has made."

Isaiah proclaimed: "The LORD comforts his people and will have compassion on his afflicted ones" (Isaiah 49:13). The apostle Paul described God as "the Father of compassion" (2 Corinthians 1:3).

God's compassion moved Jesus to delay his schedule and stand still for a social outcast. God's compassion moved Jesus to cure this weary man of his blindness. And God's compassion moves him to stop and listen to your every whisper, every moan—even every shout.

One definition of *compassion* is "a sympathetic consciousness of others' distress together with a desire to alleviate it."[3] It's one thing to feel sympathy toward someone's distress; it's quite another to feel compelled to ease that distress.

Distress is certainly a by-product of waiting. Anxiety builds as the wait drags on. Our muscles tense; our stomachs churn; we forget to smile. The angst of waiting can frazzle even the strongest soul.

God is not passively sympathetic to the distress of our waiting; his compassionate heart drives him to stop when he hears our cries. That same compassion drove him to stop and heal the lame, to stop and feed the hungry masses.

> ANXIETY BUILDS; OUR MUSCLES TENSE; OUR STOMACHS CHURN; WE FORGET TO SMILE.

His compassion also stirred him to stop and cry alongside Mary as she grieved for her dead brother Lazarus. "When Jesus saw her weeping, and the Jews who had come along with her also weeping, he was deeply moved in spirit and troubled. . . . Jesus wept" (John 11:33, 35). God weeps tears of compassion for those he loves.

The healing strength of compassion and the resiliency of the human spirit shine through in the Academy Award–winning movie *The Pianist*. The triumphant film re-creates the true story of brilliant pianist and composer Wladyslaw Szpilman during World War II.

In the film, Hitler and his German henchmen tear apart Wladyslaw's Polish Jewish family. When Wladyslaw's parents and siblings are carted off to concentration camps, he escapes and spends more than two years hiding in vacant apartments with the help of the Polish underground.

At one point no one dares even to sneak food to the holed-up musician. He is starving. Few would recognize the once dapper and fashionably dressed Wladyslaw. His dark hair has become long, stringy, and matted. His black beard is scraggly.

In the winter of 1944, a German tank pulverizes his apartment building, and the disheveled and sunken-cheeked Wladyslaw scrambles over mounds of bricks, debris, and scorched bodies to slip past the Gestapo. Mortars and machine guns boom and rattle in rapid bursts. Flames roar from bombed buildings all around him.

The dazed and frightened musician limps to the nearby remains of a house. In the barren kitchen he scavenges for any morsel of food and finally finds a large can of pickles. He desperately tries to pry it open using a stone to pound a fork through the tin. Unsuccessful, the emaciated young man cradles the can and heads upstairs to bed down for the night in the attic.

In the morning Wladyslaw attempts to tear into the pickle can with fireplace tools. After a few whacks the can thuds to the floor, leaking green juice as it rolls away. The can lands at the base of the stairway— just below a pair of black polished boots. In them stands a German captain with his holstered gun in full view.

"What are you doing here?" the officer calmly demands.

Wladyslaw shivers in fear.

"Who are you?" the German inquires. "Understand?" he adds, not knowing if the frail vagabond before him is intelligent enough to speak.

"What are you doing?" the captain asks.

"I was . . . ," the unkempt Wladyslaw stammers, "trying to open this can."

"Do you live here? Do you work here?" the German presses. "What do you do?"

"I am . . . ," Wladyslaw dryly chokes out. "I was a pianist."

"Pianist," the officer repeats before letting out a deep sigh. He motions for Wladyslaw to follow him into the next room. A regal piano sits in the spacious room, illuminated by sunlight peeking through sagging drapes.

"Play something," the German commands as he tosses his hat and coat on the piano. The virtuoso's fingers have not touched piano keys in years. He slides a dusty chair up to the instrument that once brought him fame. With grimy hands poking out from his tattered suit coat, Wladyslaw pauses.

Deep inside he whispers to his memory, hoping to squelch the wild thumping in his chest. Can he remember any of the music he once played before national audiences? Gingerly, Wladyslaw's fingers glide across the keys.

Smooth, melodious tones drift from the house into the street, where a car and driver await the German captain mesmerized by the music of the Polish pianist. How could a gruff-looking bum create such beauty through his grubby fingers?

When Wladyslaw finishes his final note, the pleased captain continues his questions and learns that Wladyslaw is a Jew and that he has been hiding in the attic. The reluctant pianist then shows the military commander the attic enclave. When the German asks if the runaway has any food, Wladyslaw proudly holds up his pickle can.

The officer walks out to his car, and Wladyslaw sinks to the floor sobbing tears of gratitude. The high-ranking Nazi could have shot his

Polish enemy on the spot or turned him over to trigger-happy soldiers. Instead, the German chose to extend compassion.

We see more offerings of compassion as the movie continues with scenes of the vacant house turned into a temporary office for the Nazi captain and his personnel. One day the commander grabs his leather satchel and heads up the stairs to the attic.

"Jew!" the captain calls out. As Wladyslaw crawls out from his hiding spot, the German tosses a package to the unshaven man. Sounds of artillery echo in the distance.

"Excuse me, please," Wladyslaw implores. "What's all the gunfire?"

About to return downstairs, the officer replies, "Russians. Across the river. All you have to do is wait a few weeks."

Just a few more weeks of waiting. If only the famished Wladyslaw can hang on. Gently, Wladyslaw lifts the newspaper-wrapped gift to his nose and inhales. Inside are a loaf of bread and a glob of jelly tucked in brown paper.

Wladyslaw scoops a dollop of jelly into his mouth and savors the sweet nourishment. Then he notices a small surprise in the package—a can opener to open his can of pickles.

In the next scene the Germans are packing up their office and driving off in trucks and cars. The captain heads back inside the house to say good-bye to his Polish friend.

"Are the Russians here?" Wladyslaw eagerly asks, taking two paper-wrapped bundles from the German.

"Not yet."

Wladyslaw peers down at the two loaves of bread he is holding in his arms.

"I don't know how to thank you," Wladyslaw says with tears forming.

"Thank God, not me," the German says. "He wants us to survive. Well," the captain adds with a slight smile, "that's what we have to believe."

The clean-shaven officer starts to leave but then stops. He looks at the once-acclaimed pianist now attired in smelly, shabby clothes with a thin blanket draped around his bony shoulders. Quickly the Nazi captain takes off his own heavy, double-breasted coat with its trademark rows of shiny silver buttons. "Take it," he says, firmly handing the coat to Wladyslaw.

With one hand Wladyslaw cradles the gift of bread; with the other he clutches the coat. Flakes of snow drift down through bomb holes in the roof. The German captain turns and walks away.[4]

For one Polish fugitive at the end of World War II, compassion came in the form of a Nazi captain who spared his life. It came in the form of a can opener, bread and jelly, and a warm winter coat.

God's compassion is incomparably greater than any acts of well-intentioned humans, even those of a cruel military officer with a change of heart. In what form do God's gifts of compassion come in your life? Are you willing to wait for them?

Dr. Martin Luther King Jr. once said, "True compassion is more than flinging a coin to a beggar."[5] Years ago my encounters with the Albanian beggars left me wondering how God models true compassion.

Now I know. He stops. He waits with us. He embraces us with gifts of compassion.

A Long Way Off

Your Loving God

There is no surprise more wonderful than the surprise of being loved; it is God's finger on man's shoulder.

Charles Morgan

Tepid rain softly splatters the streets of Metro Manila. Outside the Double Diner along Quezon Avenue, a taxi creeps into a nearby parking lot. John-John, a twenty-something man in a white T-shirt and jeans, ambles to the passenger side. As casually as his sunglasses swing from his hip pocket, John-John scrawls with his index finger on the foggy backseat window.

Raindrops twist down the glass and around John-John's crude drawings. The evil symbols, a star and triangle inside two circles, seem to say, "This is Satan's territory!" A homosexual pimp decked in a pink miniskirt and black heels sashays by and hollers "CHICKS-S-S" to entice wanton motorists. He's the "nice" man who has given several naive girls jobs.

John-John saunters back to his friends and the Filipino woman talking with them. She's a stranger, but somehow a friend—someone who really cares. Her taxi can wait.

Nothing seems to rattle this woman. Not the rain, the darkened alleys, or the fact that she's talking with pimps and prostitutes strung out on *shabu*, Filipino meth. Thelma Galvez-Nambu just hangs out with them and answers their questions about sharing IV needles and catching AIDS. This may be Satan's turf, but she's not running.

> THE EVIL SYMBOLS, A STAR AND TRIANGLE INSIDE TWO CIRCLES, SEEM TO SAY, "THIS IS SATAN'S TERRITORY!"

Just as Jesus did, Thelma befriends prostitutes. She eats with them. Hugs them. Invites them to her home. She waits without condemnation. Thelma's life revolves around these women of the night and their flesh-trade associates. She understands that the pimps, prostitutes, and patrons are just looking for love in all the wrong places.

Thelma is the counselor and spiritual director of Samaritana Transformation Ministries, Inc., an outreach to those working in Metro Manila's "entertainment industry." Many of these women—and girls—are prostitutes. Others are up-and-coming sex-trade workers. It's as though they wear oversized For Sale signs on their overused bodies.

The sex-trade industry booms in this Pacific nation of 7,107 islands, thanks in part to thousands of U.S. troops porting at Subic Bay Naval Base—troops who for years bedded Filipinos as routinely as they shined their boots. When the base closed in 1992, many of the women moved to Manila, the country's capital, and nearby Quezon City, Samaritana's headquarters.

Although prostitution is illegal in the Philippines, pimps pay bribes to police; arrested suspects seldom receive more than a vagrancy charge. Many teens flee abusive or poverty-stricken homes looking for easy pesos and adventure but end up easy prey in Manila's sexual playground.

Every day Thelma comes face-to-face with the consequences of transactional sex: Young women single-handedly supporting families, often on less than fifteen dollars per night. Teenage girls inserting catheters into their cervixes, hoping unborn babies die. Fatherless kids roaming the streets while their moms drum up business.

Yet Thelma, a native Filipino, and Jonathan, her Japanese American husband and the ministry's executive director, along with a handful of staff and volunteers, enter this carnal battlefront with optimism and tenacity. They wait for trust and friendship with the women to build. They wait for God to restore marred lives.

"These are women who will never come to us unless we come to them," Thelma told me during my visit to Manila. "Many of the women are just thrilled that we remember their names."

Thelma and her team do much more than remember names. They offer the women new career options through a vocational training program and loans for small businesses. No matter what these women are called or how deplorable their lifestyle, Thelma doesn't flinch. To her these women possess God-given worth and need to have his love expressed to them. She even named the ministry after the Tagalog word for the Samaritan woman described in the Gospel of John, chapter 4.

"This woman once had several husbands and was an outcast. No one even wanted to relate to her, but Jesus made a detour to talk to her," Thelma explained. "I was struck by his deliberate action. Jesus believed she was worthy."

Worthy and loved are two truths Thelma wants women to understand and hold on to in their own lives. So night after night she stops by seedy bars, clubs, and massage parlors in red-light districts. No environment seems to shake Thelma's calm.

She perspires in the sultry night air along Quezon Avenue and hardly notices the cars crawling along the street with hopeful johns peering and lusting, cruising for the right girl. No matter the conditions she faces, Thelma knows that introducing pimps and prostitutes to God's true love is always worth the wait.

It's been several years since I met with Thelma and her coworkers, but to me their story exemplifies the longings for pure love that cannot be bought or sold. In many ways Thelma reminds me of another woman who dared to mingle with the "least of these" along darkened streets and dank alleys.

This brave heart, Mother Teresa, said, "People throughout the world may look different or have a different religion, education, or position, but they are all the same. They are the people to be loved. They are all hungry for love. . . . Every person needs to be loved."[1]

We all hunger for love, particularly when God's apparent foot-dragging bruises our hearts and minds. God's lingering usually doesn't feel like love. Prolonged waiting confuses our emotions. One moment we feel loved, the next we feel rejected. The late Princess Diana summed up humankind's floundering in this way when she said, "The biggest disease this world suffers from in this day and age is the disease of people feeling unloved."[2]

A number of years ago I read Ernest Hemingway's World War I novel *A Farewell to Arms* and then rented the movie *In Love and War* (based on the book *Hemingway in Love and War*). In the film, Chris O'Donnell plays Ernie Hemingway, and Sandra Bullock plays the nurse who became his girlfriend, Agnes von Kurowsky.

After months of blissful romance with Agnes in Italy, Ernie must return to America. As his train pulls out, Agnes lingers on the station platform. Ernie shouts to her from the departing train car, "Tell me you love me. I need to hear you say it. Tell me."

Agnes shouts back, "I love you," and then repeats in a whisper, "I love you." But the train's shrill whistle is too loud for Ernie to hear her declaration of love.

In the following scenes Agnes takes a nursing job with a doctor in Florence. Soon she writes Ernie in America to tell him that she is considering this doctor's marriage proposal. But Agnes does not accept her boss's offer of matrimony, and eight months after the war ends, she travels to America hoping to see Ernie again. She meets war friend Harry for lunch at a New York hotel to talk about her strained relationship with Ernie.

Seated at their table, Harry says to Agnes, "Do you mind if I ask you something?"

Agnes looks up and shrugs.

"Do you love him?" Harry gently probes.

Agnes dips her head and thoughtfully nods.

"Did you ever tell him?"

Agnes looks away. Then, brown eyes brimming with tears, Agnes glances sadly at Harry. Slowly she murmurs, "Yes, but I don't think he heard me."[3]

Agnes had voiced her love to Ernie, but the deafening whistle had drowned out her message. Ernie never heard her.

At times our relationship with God is similar. He tells us he loves us, he shows us he loves us, but his "I love yous" never get through to our hearts. As we wait for one thing or another, it's as if a blaring train whistle stifles our hearing. We long for God's love, but daily pressures and distractions, hurts, and fears can keep us from hearing and believing that we are loved. We end up feeling unloved, like Ernie.

Look at King David's words in *The Message*, as he rode the tumultuous waves of waiting for God and listening for his love. In Psalm 59:10 David praised God's reliable love and punctuality: "God in dependable love shows up on time." But David also knew how it felt to plead, "Get up and come to our rescue. If you love us so much, *Help us!*" (Psalm 44:26). David was annoyed with a God who says he loves his people but seems slow to intervene on their behalf.

David's words in Psalm 31:21 remind us of God's incomparable love: "Blessed GOD! His love is the wonder of the world." So how could this man after God's own heart then speak as though he mistrusted God's love? "Don't turn your back on me just when I need you so desperately. Pay attention! This is a cry for *help*! And hurry—this can't wait!" (Psalm 102:2).

Hurry—this can't wait! Oh, that's so-o-o-o-o me at times. When it comes to waiting, I'm often like a kid who stands at the intersection punching the crosswalk button a gazillion times. Somehow the rambunctious child thinks that by incessantly pressing the button, the Walk sign will flash sooner.

Can you relate to David's roller-coaster ride of feeling loved and then unloved? Do you sometimes respond to waiting like the impatient child at a crosswalk?

When life is sailing along, you feel loved and secure; but when the harsh wind and waves of waiting sweep over you, that loving feeling sinks. And the Righteous Brothers sing your song: "You've lost that lovin' feelin'."

A love that's gone, gone, gone, is what Ken ended up with when, just before Valentine's Day 2004, Mattel announced that his romance with Barbie was over. After meeting almost forty-three years earlier on the set of a television commercial, this perfect plastic couple ended their long-term relationship.

> WE LONG FOR GOD'S LOVE, BUT DAILY PRESSURES AND DISTRACTIONS KEEP US FROM HEARING AND BELIEVING THAT WE ARE LOVED.

Some people wonder if all those bridal Barbies in toy chests around the world tired of Ken's reluctance to marry. Perhaps the ready-to-wed Barbie gave up waiting for her man to commit. Others speculate that Barbie's intimidating career path, including military medic and rock star, gave Ken even colder feet.

In breaking the news to the public, Russell Arons, Mattel's vice president of marketing, simply said that Barbie and Ken "feel it's time to spend some quality time—apart." Barbie apparently lost few tears in parting from her true love. About the time of the heavily publicized breakup, a new Cali (as in California) Barbie started sporting board shorts, bikini top, and metal hoop earrings to show off her deeper tan.

Blaine, a buff Boogie-Boarder from Australia, is now the revamped Barbie's heartthrob. As for longtime beau Ken? Arons conceded, "He will head for other waves."[4]

I'm grateful that when it comes to waiting for committed love in real life, God doesn't ask us to "head for other waves." What a relief to know that God, not some popular toy company, defines love. Unfortunately, many people eager for love jump into unhealthy relationships and compromising situations. Even those who follow God tire of waiting for his design for love to unfold.

―――――――――――――

So what is God's design for love, and how can we experience this love—especially in our love-hate relationship with waiting?

To get an accurate view of love, we need to go to the original source of love: God himself. The Bible's 1 John 4:7–10 tells us, "Dear friends, let us love one another, for love comes from God. Everyone who loves has been born of God and knows God. Whoever does not love does not know God, because God is love. This is how God showed his love among us: He sent his one and only Son into the world that we might live through him. This is love: not that we loved God, but that he loved us and sent his Son as an atoning sacrifice for our sins."

These verses quickly sum up love: God is love. Love comes from God. God showed his love by sending his Son to die for our sins. Jesus's sacrificially giving up his life is the world's greatest demonstration of love: "Greater love has no one than this, that he lay down his life for his friends" (John 15:13).

After Adam and Eve turned their backs on their loving Creator, God waited more than four thousand years for his children to accept his perfect love. Finally, he came to earth himself to draw all humankind into his loving embrace. He still waits for many of us to accept his loving gift of forgiveness and new life.

Throughout centuries and centuries of waiting, the writers of the Old Testament talked openly of God's love: "In your unfailing love you will lead the people you have redeemed" (Exodus 15:13). "He is the faithful God, keeping his covenant of love to a thousand generations of those who love him and keep his commands" (Deuteronomy 7:9). "He is good; his love endures forever" (2 Chronicles 5:13). "As high as the heavens are above the earth, so great is his love for those who fear him" (Psalm 103:11).

Just ponder for a moment these depictions of God's love. His love is unfailing. He faithfully keeps his pledge of love. His loves continues without end. His Lover is so great that it reaches far beyond the highest heavens.

One of my favorite comments by distinguished literature professor and author C. S. Lewis focuses on God's steady love for us. "On the whole, God's love for us is a much safer subject to think about than our love for him. . . . But the great thing to remember is that, though our feelings come and go, his love for us does not."[5]

God's love for us does not come and go, even when we waffle in our devotion to him during times of waiting. His love is unmovable, stable, and secure.

Jesus told a parable about a father's unfaltering love for his son. A pastor friend of mine calls this account in Luke 15:11–32 "the love story of Christianity."

The younger of two sons approaches his well-established father and asks for his inheritance in advance. The father generously grants this son his share of the family estate. Before long the restless son packs his bags and heads for a distant country. Carousing and indulging in wine and women, this young foreigner "squandered his wealth in wild living" (Luke 15:13).

The rowdy son drains his cash, his bank account, and his stock options. Too proud to wire home for more money and with a severe famine crippling the faraway country, the penniless son tumbles headlong into desperate times.

Panicked and pathetic, the former Casanova hires on for farm work with a local citizen. This citizen assigns the well-bred son of a wealthy landowner to "slop the pigs" (Luke 15:15 MSG).

Raised in the rural Midwest, I've seen and *smelled* firsthand what it means to slop the pigs. In Jesus's time and even until recent days, the common way to feed pigs was to dump out sloppy buckets of table scraps mixed with grain. To this day I can still hear those sows and piglets snorting and squealing in their mucky, reeking stalls as they hogged down their slop. (Thankfully, a large percentage of today's consumer hogs are fed wholesome grains and housed in pathogen-free, concrete-floored buildings.)

As Jesus told this story of the wayward son to the Jewish common folk and religious leaders, the very mention of pigs had to curl their toes a bit. Jews were forbidden to eat swine, which were abhorred throughout the Middle East, even by non-Jews. "The pig is also unclean; although it has a split hoof, it does not chew the cud. You are not to eat their meat or touch their carcasses" (Deuteronomy 14:8). So much for pigging out on "the other white meat."

Now that we understand the reprehensible conditions this high-rolling bachelor landed in, we can see why he is not hog wild about his new lifestyle. The former international playboy is destitute and starving for even a meager handout of pig food. But sadly, as Luke 15:16 reveals, "no one gave him anything."

He waits for some kind soul to have pity on him. He waits for crumbs and morsels to drop his way. He waits for any sign of relief from his slogging around in pigpens.

Finally, verse 17 says, "When he came to his senses . . ." The Bible doesn't tell us how long it took for this dismal prodigal to come to his senses, but I imagine once he started tending pigs, it didn't take long. Fed up with his humiliating existence, the young man determines to return to his father and beg for forgiveness. He is willing even to lay down his privileges as a son and work for hire.

Here comes my favorite part of the story. "So he got up and went to his father. But while he was still a long way off, his father saw him and was filled with compassion for him; he ran to his son, threw his arms around him and kissed him" (Luke 15:20).

While the reckless son "was still a long way off," the father sets eyes on him. The father is watching and waiting for his child to come home. What a picture of how God views us. So many times we are a "long way off" in our interactions with God and others; yet our heavenly Father gives us space while still keeping an eye on us.

Often, when we're waiting, God seems a long way off from us. But in reality we're the ones who have drifted away; we are the ones who have set our attentions elsewhere.

PANICKED AND PATHETIC, THE FORMER CASANOVA HIRES ON FOR FARMWORK WITH A LOCAL CITIZEN.

Notice the rest of verse 20. We've all seen movies and read books in which two people at odds with each other make up and joyfully join in a warm embrace. Just imagine God doing this—bolting across the fields toward his son, rushing to wrap his arms around this long-lost child.

God feels the same way about you. His compassionate love drives him to run toward you, not away from you. His unfailing, unconditional love for you does not change, even if you squander away the gifts and blessings he has freely given to you. God will never love you any more or any less than he does right now. God is your steady companion, and he's not breaking his vows of love to you.

Jesus used the parable in Luke to demonstrate a father's love, which says, "I'm still here. I'm watching for you." I encourage you to read the rest of Luke 15 to see how the father throws a feast for the youngest son, in spite of the jealous objections of the older son. The father again extends love by searching for and consoling the angry, bitter son. What a poignant example to help us see that God is not afraid of our erratic emotions and actions, particularly when we are pushed to our limits in waiting.

Less than a year before the world-renowned artist Rembrandt van Rijn died in 1669, he painted *The Return of the Prodigal Son*. This intense portrait in rich rust and gold hues is considered one of the finest biblical paintings in the world. In Rembrandt's masterpiece the wayward son from Luke 15 is on his knees before his robed father. The son buries his head into his father's chest while the father draws close the former rebellious runaway.

No matter how long the wait or if we're a long way off from the comforts of God's best for us, he is always watching and waiting for us. He is always ready to run to us with open arms of love.

Strong Shoes
Your All-Powerful God

All the strength and force of man comes from his faith
in things unseen. He who believes is strong;
he who doubts is weak.

James Freeman Clarke

The determined two-year-old plops her tiny hands on the
floor, hoists her bottom into the air, and slowly shuffles her
feet forward. Creeping along like a wobbly inchworm, Jean
Driscoll takes her first steps.

Born in 1966 with spina bifida—an imperfect closing of
the spinal column—Jean would face a bleak prognosis for her

future. Unfortunately, nearly half of all babies born in her day with spina bifida die from infection or secondary complications due to the devastating disorder.

"The doctors figured that I would never walk, never go through a regular school system, and most likely I'd be dependent on my parents my whole life," Jean says, recalling her early years. "But man's limitations are God's opportunities."

Jean takes us back to her childhood of testing man's limitations. As a toddler Jean works her way toward leg braces, determined to keep up with her older sister. Soon three younger brothers challenge Jean to fit in with the rest of the rambunctious neighborhood kids.

But it's hard to run and jump when you walk on the insides of your feet and ankles in therapeutic brown leather shoes. It's hard to fit in when the metal hinges attached to your not-so-pretty shoes squeak like rusty door hinges. It's hard to feel at ease with other kids who incessantly tease you for being the girl who walks so weird.

"I became very angry at God. I railed, 'God, why me? Why not my brothers and sister? Nobody understands!' When I would argue with my siblings, I wished my disability on them more than once," Jean admits. "I asked God repeatedly, 'What is the purpose of all of this? Why did this have to happen in the first place?'"

The childhood questions about the fairness of her disability only seem to mount as Jean struggles to march to the beat of the world around her. During a game of dodge ball in third grade, Jean snaps the tibia in her right leg. The following year she fractures her left ankle.

Waiting for bones to heal does not fit into the determined plans of this young Wisconsin girl. At age nine she teaches herself to ride a bike without training wheels, and later, in spite of a few spills and a concussion, she masters a sleek ten-speed. But a week before her fourteenth birthday, Jean rounds a corner on her bike and catches a pedal on the sidewalk. She slams down onto the pavement. Jean's dislocated hip will forever change her life.

Over the next year, the high-school freshman undergoes five major hip surgeries to correct her injuries and try to help her keep both hips in their shallow sockets. She lingers eleven months in a body cast that keeps her at home in a rented hospital bed. The waiting tortures her confused mind even more.

Two weeks after Jean's chest-to-feet cast is cut off her body, the doctor's words cut deep into her soul: "Jean is going to need to use crutches and a wheelchair to get around for the rest of her life."

The promise of eventually walking better sustained Jean through the lonely, agonizing months of recovery from her surgeries. Now the doctor's sentence shatters all her hopes of ever living an independent, active life.

"I'd gone through that whole year with foot-long scars over both hips and all those staples and all that recovery and lost time—and then none of that worked," Jean recalls. "I questioned, 'God, what is going on? What did I do? Why are you so mad at me?' I thought that having spina bifida and the surgeries not working and needing to use a wheelchair were all a result of judgment."

Brooding over her "life sentence," the teen swears to herself that she will never use crutches or a wheelchair. She yearns for her hips to support her again so she can get around with just her leg braces.

Two weeks after the doctor's grim news, Jean turns fifteen. That November day in 1981, the discouraged teen grabs a pair of crutches and ends her silent protest about adjusting to a new life. Once again defying the medical prediction that she'll be severely limited in activities, Jean returns to school using a wheelchair. She quickly rolls her way into a love for wheelchair sports.

Fast-forward a few years, and you find the young woman who once shuffled around in clunky therapeutic shoes earning a master's degree in rehabilitation administration and launching a wheelchair-racing career. The same gutsy resolve that carried her as a wobbly little girl drives Jean to train twice a day, six days a week, pushing more than one hundred miles per week in a technically designed racing chair.

In April 1990 Jean competes in her first Boston Marathon, the world's oldest and most prestigious road race. When the twenty-three-year-old snaps the finish-line tape, she surpasses the women's wheelchair-division world record by almost seven minutes!

The frustration from years of dragging her legs and enduring numerous fractures, infections, and surgeries seems to fade with each race and victory. The clenched fist that had once railed against an unfair God finally opens in grateful surrender. Jean no longer questions why she was born.

> THE FRUSTRATION FROM YEARS OF DRAGGING HER LEGS SEEMS TO FADE WITH EACH RACE AND VICTORY.

In December 1999 Jean was voted number 25 on *Sports Illustrated for Women's* "Top 100 Female Athletes of the 20th Century." On April 17, 2000, Jean became the first person ever—in any division—to win the Boston Marathon eight times.

In the 1992 and 1996 Summer Olympic Games, Jean garnered silver medals in the eight-hundred-meter women's wheelchair exhibition event. (She missed qualifying for the 2000 Olympics by .13 seconds.) In four Paralympic Games, the spunky competitor won five gold, three silver, and four bronze medals while setting three world records.

"I used to think that God was picking on me, but I was being picked out to do things that God created only me to do, and that is so humbling, so enriching," Jean said. "All the pain I went through in my younger years developed the tenacity and the mental strength that it took for me to win championship races."

Jean retired in 2000 and now works in the medical field as well as serves as a motivational speaker and corporate spokesperson. She founded Determined to Win, a nonprofit group dedicated to helping disabled people achieve their dreams and goals, particularly through sports. In all her endeavors the former world-class athlete doesn't let the accolades cloud her perspective on the true source of her strength. She ranks her relationship with God as her greatest victory.

"I look back on my challenging experiences, and I can see the nuggets of gold that have come out of them," Jean comments. "Even though there are seasons in life that seem like a never-ending winter, or a never-ending rainy season, it all is going to get balanced out once you come through that season. You've just got to put your head down and keep going."

As the overcoming Jean Driscoll knows, we have to keep going whether we're teased by friends, racked with pain, or nipped at the finish line. We have to keep going even when we're tired of waiting in seemingly never-ending winters and rainy seasons.

Scholar and author William A. Ward could have been describing Jean's amazing climb through life's disappointments and delays when he wrote, "Adversity causes some men to break; others to break records."[1] When the adverse gales of incessant waiting howl across our lives, thoughts of breaking world records are usually far from our minds. At those times most of us barely have enough energy to get out of bed in the morning, much less think about breaking records (unless we're talking about those old forty-fives collecting dust in the garage).

If you were to talk with Jean, you would quickly discover the ultimate source of her stamina to endure and thrive against all odds. Jean exemplifies the paradoxical truth of 2 Corinthians 12:10: "When I am weak, then I am strong."

Time and time again, when we face our human limitations and come to the end of ourselves, we find God upholding us with his unlimited strength. Noted American evangelist Dwight L. Moody addressed this supernatural power transfer from the Almighty: "The fact is, we have too much strength. We are not weak enough," Moody pointed out. "It is not our strength that we want. One drop of God's strength is worth more than all the world."[2]

Even one drop of God's strength will sustain us far longer than a swelling ocean's worth of our own efforts. To borrow the infamous words of Linda Richman, host of the comedic television skit "Coffee Talk," we will feel "*verklempt*" if we rely on our own puny power while we wait. The crowded waiting room of life is no place for wimps.

Maybe that's why I've always appreciated the account of mighty King Jehoshaphat when he faces thousands of brutal warriors from three tribes who came "to make war" on Judah. We pick up the war story in 2 Chronicles 20:2. "Some men came and told Jehoshaphat, 'A vast army is coming against you from Edom, from the other side of the Sea. It is already in Hazazon Tamar' (that is, En Gedi)."

These invading forces are only about twenty-five miles away from Jehoshaphat's home in Jerusalem. For many of us that's just the other side of town! Notice the king's response to this catastrophic news.

"Alarmed, Jehoshaphat resolved to inquire of the LORD, and he proclaimed a fast for all Judah. The people of Judah came together to seek help from the LORD; indeed, they came from every town in Judah to seek him" (2 Chronicles 20:3–4).

Hold it. This mighty ruler of Judah doesn't muster his armed forces to full battle alert? No. Instead, he proclaims a time of national prayer and fasting. What is he thinking! Forgoing food and talking to God is not exactly a popular battle tactic, especially with hostile adversaries rapidly advancing.

In verse 5 we find Jehoshaphat standing before his people at the Lord's temple. (I watch *The West Wing*, and I know how the president and his military advisers huddle in the war room when the nation faces an imminent security threat. But why be in a barricaded war room when you can be in the courtyard of God's house?)

Pay close attention to the opening words of Jehoshaphat's public prayer in verse 6: "O LORD, God of our fathers, are you not the God who is in heaven? You rule over all the kingdoms of the nations. Power and might are in your hand, and no one can withstand you."

Jehoshaphat demonstrates keen understanding of God's all-powerful character. This impressive king—in complete command of military legions—calls upon the master and commander of the universe. The earthly potentate acknowledges Jehovah as sovereign ruler over every kingdom and acknowledges that "no one can withstand" God's matchless power and might.

Jehoshaphat recounts past victories when God conquered Judah's enemies. The royal commander then humbly admits his inability to solve the current national crisis. In verse 12 we read, "We have no power to face this vast army that is attacking us. We do not know what to do, but our eyes are upon you."

The New American Standard Bible says, "We are powerless before this great multitude." *The Message* renders the king's words, "We're helpless before this vandal horde ready to attack us . . . we're looking to you."

Jehoshaphat admits weakness but not defeat. He faces the reality that all the king's horses and all the king's men can't keep the nation from cracking under forceful pressure from its enemies. On behalf of the entire country, Jehoshaphat confesses that he and his people are powerless and clueless.

But they know where to turn for supernatural strength. They vow to take their eyes off their problem and look to their Provider. These people of Judah understand the power in focusing on their God, whom in Hebrew they called *Elohim* (Creator God), *El Elyon* (God Most High), and *El Shaddai* (All-Sufficient One). *El* actually means "power" or "might." God's name is synonymous with strength.

Oh, how I need to remember that when I'm faint as I wait. Too often I fear that God will show up late to rescue me, so I hunker down and draw up my own battle plans. I vow to work smarter and harder, I pray a little, and then I rush ahead (fueled by a little chocolate if necessary). But in my "strength" I am pathetically vulnerable to attack.

Before we leave Jehoshaphat and his empire, let's catch God's message sent through a respected countryman named Jahaziel: "This is what the LORD says to you: 'Do not be afraid or discouraged because of this vast army. For the battle is not yours, but God's. . . . You will not have to fight this battle. Take up your positions; stand firm and see the deliverance the LORD will give you, O Judah and Jerusalem. Do not be afraid; do not be discouraged. Go out to face them tomorrow, and the LORD will be with you'" (2 Chronicles 20:15, 17).

These marching orders to Jehoshaphat and the people remind me of God's similar words earlier, to his new leader Joshua: "Have I not commanded you? Be strong and courageous. Do not be terrified; do not be discouraged, for the LORD your God will be with you wherever you go" (Joshua 1:9).

God promises his ever-present power to fight our battles for us. He directs us to stand firm while he delivers. In our war of waiting, God pulls out the heavy artillery at the precise time that he decrees—and not two days, two hours, or two seconds sooner.

A number of years ago, during an intense waiting combat over pressing finance and health concerns, I ran across a Bible verse that I turn to often, especially when I'm teetering on the edge of despondency: "Do not fear, for I am with you; do not anxiously look about you, for I am your God. I will strengthen you, surely I will help you, surely I will uphold you with My righteous right hand" (Isaiah 41:10 NASB).

God urges us not to fear or turn our heads this way and that way looking for solutions to our dilemmas of waiting. Why? Because he is with us, and he promises to strengthen, help, and uphold us.

Perhaps right now, in your own skirmish with waiting, you feel weak and flat-out exhausted. Wiped out by the tensions of holding out hope and persistently praying for your plans to come through. Although you've put up a good fight, life is truly out of your control, and you're trapped behind enemy lines. As your waiting drags on and on, you may imagine that Satan has God cornered in a dinky foxhole and now has the upper hand in the events of your life.

> TOO OFTEN I FEAR THAT GOD WILL SHOW UP LATE TO RESCUE ME, SO I HUNKER DOWN AND DRAW UP MY OWN BATTLE PLANS.

It's as if you hear the Almighty feebly plead, "Plea-s-s-s-s-e, pleas-s-s-s-s-e, Mr. Lucifer, I just can't go on. I'm so exhausted from dealing with the universe and all those people. Talk about the weight of the world on my shoulders! I absolutely have no strength left in me. I surrender all in my utter powerlessness to do anything. I sign over all the galaxies and everything in them to you."

This may sound far-fetched to you, but in reality I'll bet you've doubted God's ability to display his power in your life, especially during seasons of delay. No worries: he's used to that from his creations who are worn out from waiting.

Neglecting to wait on God started in the lush arboretum of Eden. Adam and Eve couldn't wait to bite into the fruit from the off-limits tree in the middle of the garden. Since then all their descendants—including you and me—have struggled with life's wait-and-see nature.

In 2 Corinthians 12 we find the energetic bulldozer-type apostle Paul waiting for God. A thorn in the flesh plagues Paul and interrupts his demanding speaking and traveling schedule. He has no time for such distractions and delays. Many have speculated about this "thorn" that tormented Paul. Conjectures as to the nature of Paul's suffering encompass everything from eye and stomach disorders to malaria. Whatever the source of Paul's physical limitation, it kept him from "becoming conceited" (v. 7). Being forced to slow down and wait for God's strength instead of our own is humbling.

Three times this robust go-getter from Tarsus pleads with God to remove the thorn. God, however, replies, "My grace is sufficient for you, for my power is made perfect in weakness" (v. 9).

The first time this scripture made real sense to me was the summer I spent two weeks in bed. My orthopedist ordered me to stay off my feet because the injured discs in my lower back had compressed nerves, and I had lost all feeling from my lower legs to my toes. Day after day I waited in the confines of my bedroom for the numbness to subside. Banished to my bed, I studied the weird patterns on the ceiling and the strange animals that passed by my window. I also studied God's Word.

To this day I recall those two weeks as some of the richest moments in my relationship with God. All alone in that apartment while my roommates were at work, I prayed and journaled and sang aloud to my Master Physician. Perhaps God orchestrated my thorn in the flesh to remind me that my sufficiency comes from him. In my weakness I learned afresh to lean on God's unfailing power.

Deuteronomy 33:27 declares, "The eternal God is your refuge, and underneath are the everlasting arms." Oh, how our Creator wants us to rest in his strong arms, especially when we're weak-kneed from waiting.

Near the end of the movie *The Lord of the Rings: Return of the King*, Hobbits Sam and Frodo are both weak-kneed after battling everything from that massive, deadly spider to the grotesque little Gollum. Battered and famished, the two companions collapse at the top of a ridge overlooking a valley swarming with enemy troops. Across the horizon loom the flaming fires of Mount Doom—their long-anticipated destination.

Sensing that Frodo is on the edge of giving up, Sam encourages his friend: "Come on, let's just make it down the hill for starters."[3]

That's what our empowering God says to us when we're drained and dismayed by waiting. "Let's not look too far ahead; let's just make it down this hill first."

The prophet Isaiah packed a powerhouse of truth into this passage about the mighty God who journeys beside us:

Lift your eyes and look to the heavens: Who created all these? He who brings out the starry host one by one, and calls them each by name. Because of his great power and mighty strength, not one of them is missing. . . . He gives strength to the weary and increases the power of the weak. . . . But those who hope in the LORD will renew their strength. They will soar on wings like

eagles; they will run and not grow weary, they will walk and not
be faint. (Isaiah 40:26, 29, 31)

"The universe we see when we look out to its furthest horizons
contains a hundred billion galaxies," wrote Martin Harwit in *Science*
magazine. "Each of these galaxies contains another hundred billion
stars. That's 10^{22} stars all told."[4]

The Grand Designer created the 10,000,000,000,000,000,000,000
stars and the hundred billion galaxies where they shine. That requires
colossal power way beyond our finite human capabilities to create—or
even our intelligence to comprehend. Not only did God design the 10^{22}
stars, but he also gave each individual star a name. And his supreme rule
of the universe doesn't stop there. He knows the precise whereabouts
of every one of the multibillion stars, including those falling stars we
wish upon.

With these unparalleled credentials on his résumé, it's no wonder
God can easily "give strength to the weary" so we can "run and not grow
weary . . . walk and not be faint." We need the herculean fortitude of
our God to defend and uphold us when we're detained or set adrift by
life's unpredictable ways.

As a kid I loved watching superhero TV cartoons with my two brothers.
Mighty Mouse and Superman were always favorites, and we can't forget
Batman. To this day I can still see Popeye, the Sailor Man, leaping to a
two-fisted scuffle with Brutus. Popeye's mantra, "I'm strong to the finich,
'cause I eats my spinach," did not spur me to eat canned spinach, but it
did make me ponder about brawny heroes saving the day.

Today, as a grown woman, I know that heroic strength goes deeper
than flexing beefy biceps. Samson sported those, and look where it got
him—blind with a bad haircut and crushed under a collapsed building
(Judges 16). Yes, he may well be the first biblical figure who truly
suffered from a bad hair day.

As an elite Olympic athlete, Jean Driscoll trained day after day to build sinewy biceps and a well-muscled upper body so she could conquer countless miles of downward strokes on her racing wheelchair. Yet with all her incredible physical stamina, Jean discovered that her competitive edge, both on and off the racecourse, came through spiritual strength that only God could supply.

Part of God's spiritual conditioning program for all of us is a workout in waiting. Waiting conditions our flabby faith and tones our prayer life. Waiting stretches our belief in our invincible God. Waiting pushes us to the limits when we think we can't go on. Waiting equips us to "be strong in the Lord and in his mighty power" (Ephesians 6:10).

Early nineteenth-century poet Felicia Hemans said, "Strength is born in the deep silence of long-suffering hearts." In the deep silence of a long-suffering heart that waits, God engenders strength. Are you currently waiting in a deep silence of the heart? Do you long for God to support you with his strong arms?

As you wait in the stillness, let the psalmist's words whisper hope into your soul. "I would have despaired unless I had believed that I would see the goodness of the Lord in the land of the living. Wait for the Lord; be strong and let your heart take courage; yes, wait for the Lord" (Psalm 27:13–14 NASB).

Dutch watchmaker Corrie ten Boom could have written these verses instead of King David. Licensed in 1922 as the first female watchmaker in Holland, Corrie enjoys a promising career until the Nazis arrest her entire family for hiding fugitives during World War II. Imprisoned for nearly a year, Corrie and her sister Betsie suffer in horrendous conditions. They wait with great courage for God to deliver them once again to "the land of the living."

Betsie dies at Germany's Ravensbrook concentration camp a few days before Christmas 1944. Shortly after, Corrie is handed a card stamped *entlassen*, which means "released." On December 31 she steps back into freedom. Only later does Corrie learn that her release was a mistake. All the women of her age at the camp were killed the week after she was set free. But Corrie's release was no mistake in God's plan.

Imprisoned for doing good and saving lives, this courageous woman waited and waited through months and months of abuse, injustice, and sorrow. Undergirded by her "refuge and strength" (Psalm 46:1), Corrie walked out of that deathtrap stronger than ever. Fortified by the sustaining strength of her all-powerful God, Corrie could proclaim, "If God sends us on stony paths, he provides strong shoes."[6]

None of us can predict the stony paths of waiting that we will travel in life. Sometimes we will stumble on these rocky roads; other times we'll collapse near the ditch, too tired and discouraged to take another step.

That's when God sits down beside us and laces up his strong shoes on our achy, blistered feet. Taking our hand in his, he reassures us: "Come on, let's just make it down the hill for starters."

Smiling in the Rain

Your Gentle God

God tempers the wind to the shorn lamb.

Henri Estienne

I confess. I once crawled into a back-alley dumpster scavenging for treasure. A rusty steel garbage bin sitting in the shadows between a gas station and a tavern. I strained against the massive lid and eased myself into that trash-filled monstrosity—on a Sunday afternoon, no less. Call me a thief and a Sabbath breaker.

A bone-chilling, drenching rain complicated my escapade. It's hard to gain footing in a dumpster when your mud-packed tennis shoes are slipping on plastic garbage bags. Fortunately, I was sliding around on closed bags and not some mound of rank trash. Still, since both a tavern and gas station shared this refuse pile, I knew that with one slip, I'd be floundering in a smelly mix of oily car parts, slick beer bottles, and greasy French fries.

Was I a wild teen on an I-dare-you challenge? No. I was a forty-one-year-old church deaconess on a mission of mercy. And I had an unlikely accomplice in my back-alley adventure: my father. A respected businessman, former church treasurer, and town mayor for sixteen years.

WHY WOULD AN ELDERLY COMMUNITY LEADER JOIN HIS GROWN DAUGHTER IN RANSACKING A DUMPSTER IN THE MIDDLE OF THE DAY?

Why would an elderly community leader join his grown daughter in ransacking a dumpster in the middle of the day, in the middle of a downpour? Even less intelligent thieves wouldn't choose to attack under such unfavorable circumstances.

Well, it's really Dad's fault. Trust me. Grief has a way of fogging up your mind. Our family had just endured my mother's lingering death from a massive stroke. She died at 2 a.m., and by roughly 2 p.m. Dad and I were hitting the back alleys.

Reeling from the loss of Mom and loss of sleep, Dad let my sister-in-law Linda and me clean out some of Mom's things. In our own dazed grief, we tossed some items on the kitchen counter into the trash.

At one point Linda held up a mauve plastic container with a bottom partial denture inside. It looked like an old set of Mom's false teeth, so

Linda asked Dad if we could just pitch them. Dad nodded, and we kept on tidying the kitchen. On the way to the funeral home to pick out Mom's casket, we added about a half-dozen crammed-full garbage bags to the refuse bin behind my father's gas station.

Not until hours later did we realize Dad's blunder. The dentures were his, not my mother's.

Thus began our dumpster outing in a rainstorm. Wobbling in the odoriferous bin, I'd hand a couple of garbage bags to Dad, and he'd fling them in the back of his pickup truck. We'd drive the three blocks to his house and sit in the garage, in our drenched clothes, opening each bag and searching for the dentures.

After two hours and three slippery trips to the dumpster, we finally found my father's teeth buried at the bottom of a hefty garbage bag—nestled securely inside that infamous mauve case.

All the while I just knew my mother was up in heaven smiling at us. For years she had told Dad to wear his dentures and not leave them by the kitchen sink. The afternoon of dumpster-diving gave my father and me a distraction from our grief that we could literally sink our teeth into. Fortunately, that dreary March day God touched our family with his gentleness—a brush of levity when we needed it most.

We all need God's gentleness when we're slammed by the harsh realities of life . . . or death . . . and we're left to wait for relief. We need to experience the soft, tender side of our Creator when distressing circumstances threaten our patience and strong-arm us into waiting even longer.

A Congolese proverb asks, "The teeth are smiling, but is the heart?"[1] How light is your heart these days? Has the merry-go-round of waiting spun you around one too many times, causing you to reel in confusion and dismay?

If you're like me, waiting for God to act sometimes makes me feel he is unkind and stern. Sometimes my view of God distorts to the point where I see him as a gruff ogre rather than a tenderhearted friend. When I reach this level of misunderstanding, I must return to what I know is absolutely true: God is gentle, and he longs to reassure us with his gentleness.

One of my favorite examples of God's gentleness is found in the Old Testament story of Elijah, the prophet who, with God's fiery help, displays an amazing pyrotechnic miracle that literally brings the nation of Israel to its knees. For the grand finale, Elijah orders the execution of the 450 prophets of Baal (1 Kings 18:16–46). This totally ticks off Queen Jezebel, who already has her claws sharpened to get this "renegade" man of God.

To better understand the harsh spiritual and moral climate of Elijah's day, we need to look at the lifestyle of Israel's royal family. In 1 Kings 16:30 and 33 we read a sober account of the king of Israel, Ahab, and his diabolical character: "Ahab son of Omri did more evil in the eyes of the LORD than any of those before him. . . . and did more to provoke the LORD, the God of Israel, to anger than did all the kings of Israel before him."

Ahab's choice of women contributes greatly to his evil reputation. He marries Jezebel, the daughter of Ethbaal, king of Sidon and Tyre. Steeped in the religious traditions of worshiping Baal, a Phoenician sun-god, Jezebel persuades her husband to serve the god of her homeland. So in his kingdom that predominantly worshiped Jehovah, Ahab erects a grand temple with an altar to honor Baal.

Queen Jezebel even allows 450 prophets of Baal and four hundred prophetesses of the Canaanite goddess Asherah to dine at her table. Most likely these were Jezebel's cultish recruits and a source of national pride for the first lady.

Exercising more of her political clout, depraved Jezebel orders the murder of many of God's prophets (1 Kings 18:13). Some scholars refer to Jezebel as the first female religious persecutor. Call her a female Adolph Hitler, Idi Amin, or Saddam Hussein for killing her own people. No one dared mess with Jezebel, not even King Ahab, who seemed usually to acquiesce to his wicked wife.

So along comes Elijah, a Tishbite from the hill country of Gilead, to announce to his majesty Ahab that a massive drought will strike Israel. Can't you just see Ahab and Jezebel squirming on their thrones at this man of God's words? "As the LORD, the God of Israel, lives, whom I serve, there will be neither dew nor rain in the next few years except at my word" (1 Kings 17:1).

No moisture on the land except at Elijah's word. But Elijah is not speaking on his own behalf—he represents the King of kings, the divine ruler of heaven and earth. The battle lines are drawn in the sunbaked ground between this bold prophet and the notoriously corrupt Ahab and Jezebel.

True to Elijah's prediction, no dew or rain falls on Israel for three and a half years. That's a long time to wait for a cloudy day. The bone-dry months and years parch the souls of the Israelites. Jezebel's heart toward God likely shrivels even more.

By the time Elijah challenges Jezebel's false prophets on Mount Carmel to prove the supernatural power of Baal and then kills them all (1 Kings 18:16–40), Jezebel is royally irate. She puts out a hit on Elijah, calling for his death within twenty-four hours.

If anyone ever needed a touch of gentleness, it is Elijah. This man of God has confronted the barbarous leaders of the land, a couple acting with cruelty and motivated by vengeance. Kind, soft-hearted, genteel, amiable, and meek are not words to describe this dastardly duo.

No one can fault Elijah for getting out of Dodge. "Elijah was afraid and ran for his life," says 1 Kings 19:3. Terrified and alone, Elijah hightails it south to the desert of Judah. He collapses under a broom tree or juniper bush, which can grow up to twelve feet tall in that region.

There, under the branches of a bush, Elijah slumps, exhausted and dejected. He cries out to God: "'I have had enough, LORD,' he said. 'Take my life; I am no better than my ancestors'" (1 Kings 19:4).

In life's disruptions it's natural to blurt out, "God, I've had enough!" When I was little, my brothers would playfully tickle me under the arms. When I couldn't stand the torture anymore, they would stop and let me go if I cried uncle. Recently, in one of my logjams of waiting, I screamed aloud to God, "Uncl-l-l-l-le!" I figured I'd try this game of surrender with him. I didn't experience immediate relief from my waiting, but it felt good to yell for a few seconds. And I'm sure I made God chuckle a little.

Yet life's wait-and-see experiences are no laughing matter. Waiting for God to intervene when we need him most can drive us to despair. Sometimes, like Elijah, in our weariness we just want God to take us directly to heaven. Sometimes, in the midst of protracted delays, life just seems too burdensome to put one foot in front of the other.

Elijah did what most of us need to do when we reach this point of despondency while waiting. He took a nap. Rest may not immediately bring our long-awaited promises or the changes we hoped for, but it can soothe our frayed nerves and strengthen our fatigued spirits.

I love what happens next with the snoozing Elijah. "All at once an angel touched him and said, 'Get up and eat.' He looked around, and there by his head was a cake of bread baked over hot coals, and a jar of water. He ate and drank and then lay down again" (1 Kings 19:5–6).

Right in the middle of the desolate desert, the angel of the Lord gently touches his servant. This angel is no ordinary cherub; this most likely is a Christophany, or the appearance of Jesus Christ. Jesus himself comes to earth to care for his distraught servant Elijah. Gently, the Lord nudges his fallen warrior and leaves him a hot loaf of fresh sourdough and a chilled bottle of Perrier. With the refreshments right by his head, Elijah doesn't even have to get up. He can just roll over, nibble, sip, and continue his siesta.

Isn't this just like our God? Right when we're ready to waste away in our waiting, God touches us with his gentle presence. Perhaps it's an encouraging phone call or e-mail from a friend. A dinner invitation from a neighbor. An unexpected gift of money. A joyful hug from your child.

There's no limit to the number of ways God chooses to extend his gentleness. And often he'll show up in our season of struggle in ways we least expect. This happens to Elijah. The angel of the Lord delivers food and water to Elijah a second time, and strengthened by that food, the prophet travels forty days and nights until he

> SOMETIMES, LIKE ELIJAH, IN OUR WEARINESS WE JUST WANT GOD TO TAKE US DIRECTLY TO HEAVEN.

reaches a cave at Mount Horeb. There God speaks to Elijah and sends him to stand on the mountain. Elijah is to wait for God to pass by.

A powerful wind tears the mountains apart and shatters rocks all around. But God is not in this roaring wind. Elijah waits.

Next, a violent earthquake rumbles across the mountain. Yet the Lord does not appear before Elijah. Elijah waits.

Soon a fire rages near the prophet, but God still does not reveal himself in the flames. Elijah waits.

Finally, 1 Kings 19:12–13 says, "After the fire came a gentle whisper. When Elijah heard it, he pulled his cloak over his face and went out and stood at the mouth of the cave. Then a voice said to him, 'What are you doing here, Elijah?'"

Like Elijah, in our waiting we may expect God to march into our circumstances and dramatically turn the tables. We may not expect the Almighty to show up in windstorms, earthquakes, and fires, but we'd sure like him to come galloping in on a sinewy white steed (like the one Gandalf rides in the Lord of the Rings movies).

During life's drawn-out adventures, we want to believe that God will at least poke his head into our lives. We want him to end our waiting—to cure illnesses, change people's hearts, overthrow governments, and bless us with peace and prosperity.

But if we're holding out for God to conform to our expectations and desires, our wait will only persist. I appreciate the insights of Max Lucado as written in his book *In the Eye of the Storm*: "Because we look for the bonfire, we miss the candle. Because we listen for the shout, we miss the whisper. But it is in burnished candles that God comes, and through whispered promises he speaks."[2]

In our delays, postponements, and slowdowns, may we never miss the gentle whisper of our God. When I ponder how God whispers gently in my life, I think of one year in particular when I endured intense, daily back and leg pain. On some of my worst days, my coworker and close friend Julie would sneak up behind me as I sat in my office and surprise me by pressing her cheek against mine. These cheek hugs were a tender reminder of God's gentleness to me.

In your anguish of waiting, you need God to press his face against yours to reassure you that he is present and that he cares. Waiting can pummel your faith and shred your view of God. Waiting can also surprise you with God's gentle whisper and his soothing touch. Shh-h-h . . . can you hear God in your life today? Can you sense his gentle presence?

As I write these words, I glance at a magazine on my desk that shows a gripping photo of a nurse's aide tenderly towel drying the skin of an AIDS patient covered with large Kaposi's sarcoma (KS) lesions.

The patient in the photo is Dave Cruver, whom I visited in his hospice room. Dave was one of dozens of people I met during a two-month investigation into how Christians are caring for AIDS patients around the world. That magazine assignment radically changed my view of hurting people and my view of God's gentleness.

I'll never forget my first few moments with Dave in Denver's Hospice of Saint John. He meticulously unwrapped twisted, matted gauze from his foot. His scaly, purplish toes were the size of cigar stubs. A fungus feasted on the blood in his veins. The blackish purple splotches of KS covered his body—the end of his nose, his cheeks, his chest, his legs. This was AIDS in all its debilitating glory.

"In the Bible they talk about the spots of leprosy, and sometimes I wonder if this KS is like that," Dave told me as he scratched a lesion below the black-widow tattoo on his arm. Before another dose of morphine, Dave reflected on his journey with AIDS.

"I have to have faith in God," Dave said. "I need him to be by my side for strength. I'm not really scared of dying. I'm more scared of the pain before I die. I just wish I had something they could cure with a couple of antibiotics."

The hours I spent with this thirty-seven-year-old man weeks before he died introduced me to the tangible gentleness of God through caring hospice volunteers and staff. The photograph of the nurse's aide carefully holding Dave's head while she dried off his lesion-covered skin is a true picture of God gently caring for us in our times of greatest need.

Perhaps Dave was right about his KS being like the spots of leprosy mentioned in the Bible. The way AIDS patients are often shunned today is similar to the way lepers of Bible times were cast aside. Ancient Jews declared lepers unclean and banished the afflicted from their communities in accordance with Levitical law: "As for the leper who has the infection, his clothes shall be torn, and the hair of his head shall be uncovered, and he shall cover his mustache and cry, 'Unclean! Unclean!' . . . He shall live alone; his dwelling shall be outside the camp" (Leviticus 13:45–46 NASB).

Throughout history people from all cultures have feared this dreaded disease. In medieval times priests read a burial service over lepers before they were banished from the city. Many medieval lepers lived in vast leprosaria built by nobles. Beginning in the 1860s, Hawaiians ordered their lepers to live on the island of Molokai. This practice ended in 1969, but several of the leper patients asked to remain in the settlement for life.

> IT WAS ONE THING FOR JESUS TO PRONOUNCE, "BE CLEAN," AND QUITE ANOTHER TO TOUCH THIS MAN OF TATTERED BODY AND SOUL.

Properly known as Hansen's Disease, leprosy is caused by a bacillus, and in severe cases it results in skin nodules and ulcers that spread. These lesions can lead to loss of sensation and deformity. Today, leprosy is largely confined to a few countries of the world and is effectively treated with a cocktail of modern drugs.

But in Jesus's day, anyone suffering from leprosy endured a miserable life as a pariah. These individuals were condemned to live away from their families and the rest of the community while waiting for a cure or death. Many days lepers waited even for a faraway glimpse of a healthy human being.

In Luke 5:12–15 we read of Jesus's encounter with a man covered with leprosy. When this desperate leper saw Jesus, the man fell on his face and implored Jesus to heal him. No doubt covered with oozing sores and disfigured by his disease, this man fell to the dirt before the Master Physician. He could not wait another day, another minute. He knew his only hope was in God.

How about us? When we're sick of waiting, where do we turn? To other people, to busyness, to any pleasure that masks our impatience? By approaching Jesus, this spurned outcast risked punishment, for he crossed the health boundaries imposed between lepers and "clean" people. Yet the leper went straight to God with his angst and pain. He didn't care what others would think.

Do you know how Jesus responded to this untouchable, a man who perhaps had not come close to a healthy person in years? A man who likely longed for the feeling of a hug, a soft touch on his arm, a kiss on his cheek. Luke 5:13 describes the moment Jesus turned his attention to this exiled leper: "Jesus reached out his hand and touched the man. 'I am willing,' he said. 'Be clean!' And immediately the leprosy left him."

It was one thing for Jesus to pronounce, "Be clean," and quite another to touch this man of tattered body and soul. Jesus broke the rigid Jewish ceremonial laws by placing his hand on the unclean castoff. But God is never confined to religious rules.

In this story we see the gentleness of God overriding letter-of-the-Law restrictions. This is the same God who says, "Come to me, all you who are weary and burdened, and I will give you rest. Take my yoke upon you and learn from me, for *I am gentle* and humble in heart, and you will find rest for your souls. For my yoke is easy and my burden is light" (Matthew 11:28–30, emphasis added).

Saint Augustine spoke highly of these verses when he said, "I have read in Plato and Cicero sayings that are very wise and very beautiful; but I never read in either of them: 'Come unto me all ye that labour and are heavy laden.'"[3]

God is gentle, and he offers us rest when we are weary and burdened by waiting. He invites us to come to him when we feel like we're franticly slogging around in a rain-soaked dumpster or ready to dry up in the desert. He longs to touch us with his gentleness, even if we are outcasts with leprosy or AIDS.

I find great comfort in knowing that our God is a gentle shepherd—regardless of the condition he finds us in on any given day. One of my favorite verses, Isaiah 40:11, portrays the tender relationship between God and his lambs: "He tends his flock like a shepherd: He gathers the lambs in his arms and carries them close to his heart; he gently leads those that have young."

In his inspiring book *A Shepherd Looks at Psalm 23*, Phillip Keller shares his experiences as a sheep rancher and the parallels to the Good Shepherd's care. When I think of Keller's insightful writing, one illustration stands out in my mind. Keller wrote about "cast" sheep, which is an old English shepherd's term for a sheep that has rolled over on its back and can't get up by itself.

"A 'cast' sheep is a very pathetic sight. Lying on its back, its feet in the air, it flays away franticly struggling to stand up, without success. Sometimes it will bleat a little for help, but generally it lies there lashing about in frightened frustration."[4]

As the sheep struggles on its back, gases build up in the stomach, and blood circulation is cut off from the extremities. The shepherd must continually search for such struggling, helpless sheep and set them on their feet again, or they can die within hours.

Many times, in waiting, we're just like a cast sheep, toppled over on the ground and frantically flailing in all our self-effort. The harder we try to right our lives, the weaker we get. We are stuck and thrashing about in frightened frustration. Only our Good Shepherd can rescue us from our predicament.

Not long ago I saw this happen with my aging dog Kinzey, who was hobbled by hip dysplasia and arthritis. Kinzey was outside, and I opened the front door to let him back in the house. When I looked into the yard, I saw four hairy white legs kicking in the evergreen bushes at the side of the front steps.

Kinzey had slipped coming up the steps and rolled over the edge. Helplessly wedged between the steps and the thick bushes, Kinzey looked like a cast sheep (he was a Shetland sheepdog). The poor pooch couldn't work his way out of his vulnerable position. He needed me to squeeze down into the scratchy bushes beside him and gently pull him out of the small space where he was trapped. Once I got my bewildered dog back on his feet, I gingerly pulled the prickly needles from his face and coat.

That's what God does with us. He slips in beside us when we're cast down, and he gently helps us to our feet. Tenderly he stays with us until we regain our strength and can walk again without wobbling.

When we stagger and stumble as we wait, our Good Shepherd soothingly gathers us in his arms, carries us close to his heart, and gently leads us onward. As we wait, there's no better place to rest.

Open Hands
Your Merciful God

I have always found that mercy bears richer fruits
than strict justice.

Abraham Lincoln

In the classic *Seinfeld* episode featuring the Soup Nazi, Kramer
and Jerry introduce their sidekicks to a tiny New York City deli
that serves the grumpy owner's irresistible soup. Eager to order
the scrumptious crab bisque, Elaine nonchalantly saunters up
to the deli counter and makes eye contact with the stone-faced
owner-chef, dubbed the Soup Nazi by certain patrons.

Flashing her charming, girlish smile, Elaine slaps her hands on the steel counter above the steamy soups. The dark, mustachioed chef stares back coldly. Elaine eagerly inquires with a confident air, "Did anyone tell you, you look like Al Pacino? You know, Al Pacino in *Scent of a Woman*."

Elaine leans toward the owner and launches into a husky-voiced imitation of Pacino's character: "Whoooo-ahhhhhhhhh . . . Whoooo-ahhhhhhhhh!"

The Soup Nazi grimaces and abruptly yells, "NO SOUP FOR YOU! COME BACK, ONE YEAR!"

Sometimes I see God as the Soup Nazi. "No answered prayer for you! Wait much, much longer. Come back, one year!" At least that's how I've viewed him lately. No cure for my dad's cancer. No immediate answers to my own health quandaries. No new clients. No husband. Come back, one year.

Maybe you can relate. No baby. No extra income. No friends who truly understand. No new car. No change of heart in your teen. No fitting in at church.

WHEN IMPATIENCE FESTERS, WE OFTEN CONCLUDE THAT GOD IS INSENSITIVE.

You get the picture. Waiting for God to show up in our pressing everyday problems does not always help his reputation. If we didn't know better, we'd swear some days that God is a cruel chef refusing to feed his starving children. As we wait, we may reason, *OK, God—forget the scrumptious crab bisque. I'd settle for some simple broth.*

When impatience festers, we often conclude that God is insensitive and cross; kind of a celestial Soup Nazi. A story in Willa Cather's classic novel *O Pioneers!* illustrates the way some of us look at God.

Alexandra Bergson is the central character of this book about the stalwart frontier people taming the wind-blasted prairie of Nebraska. Alexandra hosts a wedding at her spacious farmhouse for one of her Swedish house girls, Signa, and Nelse, one of the Norwegian hired men. After the wedding supper, Ivar, Alexandra's longtime hand, hitches horses to a wagon to take the bride and groom to their new home on Alexandra's north quarter. Alexandra's youngest brother, Emil, and neighbor Marie Shabata carry wedding presents to the wagon while Alexandra finds Signa to say good-bye and leave her with some motherly counsel.

[Alexandra] was surprised to find that the bride had changed her slippers for heavy shoes and was pinning up her skirts. At that moment Nelse appeared at the gate with the two milk cows that Alexandra had given Signa for a wedding present.

Alexandra began to laugh. "Why, Signa, you and Nelse are to ride home. I'll send Ivar over with the cows in the morning."

Signa hesitated and looked perplexed. When her husband called her, she pinned her hat on resolutely. "I ta-ank I better do yust like he say," she murmured in confusion.

Alexandra and Marie accompanied Signa to the gate and saw the party set off, old Ivar driving ahead in the wagon and the bride and groom following on foot, each leading a cow. . . .

"I've no patience with Signa, marrying that grumpy fellow!" Marie declared. "I wanted her to marry that nice Smirka boy who worked for us last winter. I think she liked him, too."

"Yes, I think she did," Alexandra assented, "but I suppose she was too much afraid of Nelse to marry any one else. . . . We're a terribly practical people, and I guess we think a cross man makes a good manager."[1]

Some of us consider God a cross fellow who would make us yank on our boots, pin up our skirts, and trudge across lumpy fields pulling a couple of stubborn cows—on our wedding night! In our season of delays, we may resign ourselves to serving a God who we think "makes a good manager" but remains detached from our true feelings and deepest needs. We see him as hardhearted and unmerciful.

Yet this is not how the Bible describes God. The NIV Bible uses the word *mercy* 129 times, and most of those incidents refer to God's character. Throughout the Bible we find God's people boasting of his mercy. Nehemiah declared, "In your great mercy you did not put an end to them or abandon them, for you are a gracious and merciful God" (Nehemiah 9:31). David asserted, "His mercy is very great" (1 Chronicles 21:13) and, "Remember, O LORD, your great mercy and love, for they are from of old" (Psalm 25:6).

The prophet Micah exclaimed, "Who is a God like you, who pardons sin and forgives the transgression of the remnant of his inheritance? You do not stay angry forever but delight to show mercy" (Micah 7:18).

God delights to show us mercy. I like that. The apostle Paul said that God "is rich in mercy" (Ephesians 2:4), and later, "The Lord is full of compassion and mercy" (James 5:11). God is lavishly merciful.

When it comes to God's mercy, either the Bible has it wrong or we do. I'm sticking with God's Word on this one. Countless people through the ages have testified to God's mercy, and I'm one of them. In the words of famed seventeenth-century poet and playwright Thomas Otway, "Mercy's indeed the attribute of heaven."[2]

A number of years ago, during the hostile fighting between Rwanda's Hutus and Tutsis, I was asked to interview Winnie Babihuga, a Ugandan relief manager for World Vision who was living in a camp with eighteen thousand displaced Rwandans. After our trans–Atlantic telephone conversation, I sat in my office and could not eat my lunch.

Winnie's story did more than quell my appetite; it confirmed my understanding of God's mercy.

In spring of 1994 Winnie moved from her native Uganda to the chilly hills of northern Rwanda to bring supplies and spiritual aid to the thousands of Rwandans fleeing the barbaric rampage of Rwanda's warring government and rebel army troops. Several news sources confirm that roughly one million Tutsis and Hutus had been slaughtered.

Winnie spoke of frail-boned children whacked with machetes like stew meat being chopped by a butcher. Jeremiah 6:23 describes assailants like this as inhumane people who "are cruel and show no mercy."

"Some of the children lost their arms, legs, and ears trying to protect themselves," Winnie said. She told me about seven-year-old Marietta, who watched attackers slash her parents to death. Winnie also described how two little sisters crawled under piles of rotting corpses to escape murder. For weeks thousands of bloated bodies, many of them babies, drifted down the Kagera River, stockpiling in Uganda's Lake Victoria.

Winnie also warned me that for those who survived the bloodlust, the threat of death still lurked nearby. Starvation, cholera, typhoid, dysentery, malaria, and pneumonia plagued the hollow-eyed Rwandans crammed into makeshift camps. Thousands of people no longer had relatives or a place to call home. And for most, the memories of watching their loved ones mercilessly hacked and stabbed to death left scars deeper than those on their bodies.

In the middle of the Rwandan melee, a number of courageous Christians like Winnie risked their own lives to care for the people trapped in a tribal slaughter of countrymen turning on each other like ravenous wolves.

"There are thousands of people who are helpless in Rwanda, and if nobody stays with them, their hope diminishes," Winnie explained.

"Our being there helps them know that somebody is standing by them."

Being there when hope diminishes. Standing by with relief and aid when brutality strips defenseless people of normalcy, love, and safety. Extending care even to the murderers who don't deserve help. That's mercy.

Winnie told me that as she waited for the cruelties of war to end, she often read God's words about loving her neighbors, the Rwandans south of her homeland. She talked to God about helping her to respond with mercy and compassion even to the assassins. It's obvious that Winnie understood God's heart.

God doesn't expect us to be an Oscar Schindler, who saved Jews in World War II, or a Mother Teresa, who saved the poor of India. Nor does he expect us to be aid worker Winnie Babihuga. But God does want us to be like him, "to love mercy and to walk humbly" with him (Micah 6:8).

Author Sherwood Wirt offered a poignant definition of mercy: "Mercy is unmerited favor from God himself to an erring people who can do nothing to earn it except to hold out their hands."[3]

I've heard mercy defined as "God not giving us what we deserve." All of us deserve punishment for our rebellious thoughts and wayward actions. We are all guilty of sin, which warrants a death sentence. But our merciful Judge put down the gavel against us and, instead, sent Jesus to suffer on a cross and die in our place.

Daniel 9:9 states: "The Lord our God is merciful and forgiving, even though we have rebelled against him." And the apostle Peter exclaimed, "Praise be to the God and Father of our Lord Jesus Christ! In his great mercy he has given us new birth into a living hope through the resurrection of Jesus Christ from the dead" (1 Peter 1:3).

In his book *God: Discover His Character*, Bill Bright wrote, "God's mercy is an attribute that leads him to show compassionate concern for his people and tenderhearted treatment of the needy. . . . In the supreme act of mercy, God displayed divine favor and forbearance to us guilty offenders. He took our punishment upon himself."[24]

Just the other day I realized afresh how much I am a guilty offender. I chomp at the bit when I have to wait in lines longer than a few minutes. With twenty-five checkout lanes at most superstores, you'd think they would keep at least half of them open during busy shopping hours. But no-o-o-o-o!

> BEING THERE WHEN HOPE DIMINISHES. THAT'S MERCY.

Being tall, I enjoy the advantage of peering over the magazine and candy racks near the cash registers to spot the shortest checkout lines in a store. I'm not afraid to bolt to another line if I think it will save me from thumbing through those sensationalized tabloids. (Why are all the best home-decorating and fashion magazines stacked at the front of the line, where you're supposed to start unloading your cart?)

So there I am on a midweek run to the crowded superstore with those unbeatable prices. I spot a short line with the cashier's light still on. One woman is writing out her check, and the elderly woman behind her has fewer than fifteen items. I halfway smirk at the bored people in long lines a couple of registers away. I wheel my cart behind the gray-haired woman, but not so close as to invade her personal checkout space.

Painstakingly the woman pulls each item from her cart and arranges them neatly on the black conveyor belt. I glance at the tabloids plastered with huge out-of-focus photos depicting Hollywood stars at their worst.

As the grandmotherly woman continues to caress each can, jar, and toilet-paper package with care, I edge my cart a little closer. *I'm almost out of here!* I gloat to myself.

Just then the aged shopper lifts the Closed Lane sign from behind her purse in the cart. "Oh, I guess I forgot to set that down," she says in a faint, quivering voice.

I roll my eyes at this customer's carelessness and immediately appeal to the cashier. "Excuse me, I've been in this line a while, and the Closed Lane sign wasn't out. When I pulled up, your light was still on."

"This lane is closed. This woman is my last customer," the cashier blandly replies without looking my way.

I am not pleased with the cashier's lifeless attitude or the elderly woman's mistake. Because of these two blundering people, I am forced to hunt for a new line and start my wait all over again. Grr-r-r.

Believe me, I felt they both deserved to be scolded and the cashier reprimanded for her poor customer service. I complained to a fellow customer in my new line and even told my new cashier about the incident, but it did little to assuage my spirit of revenge.

As I walked across the parking lot, still fuming indignantly about waiting longer than I should have, I sensed God tugging at my heart. At this point I felt more maniacal than merciful. But I confessed my desire to settle the score and asked for God to calm my heart. So much for my stint as the Shopping Nazi. No short lines for you! Old lady, come back one year! Cashier, you're fired!

Waiting sure elicits the not-so-lovely from our minds and hearts. Just ask David—the unknown harp-playing shepherd boy who becomes the greatest ruler of Israel. Once God rejects King Saul as Israel's king and David is anointed as his future replacement, King Saul descends into an emotional and spiritual quagmire. Saul festers with worry and jealousy as he waits for his reign to end, and David is frequently the target of the king's wrathful impatience—even as David himself waits for God to fulfill his promise.

David serves as Saul's personal musician to help soothe the troubled king's tortured mind: "The Spirit of the Lord had departed from Saul, and an evil spirit from the Lord tormented him" (1 Samuel 16:14).

Then David defeats Goliath, Israel's enemy, but he still has to wait to lead Israel. In Saul's disturbed mental state, on several occasions he attempts to kill David with a spear. David doesn't retaliate but rather waits for God to act on his behalf. David waits for Saul's daughter Merab's hand in marriage, but Saul gives her to another man. David then waits to marry Saul's younger daughter, Michal, but Saul first requires David to kill one hundred Philistines as a dowry. Overachieving David kills two hundred.

Nothing seems to please the agitated King Saul. So David waits. When Saul sends hit men to stake out David and Michal's house, David flees to Ramah. A marked man, David remains on the run for years. He holes up in a cave and waits for God's direction. He becomes a Robin Hood, of sorts. As 1 Samuel 22:2 tells us, "All those who were in distress or in debt or discontented gathered around him, and he became their leader. About four hundred men were with him."

The king-to-be is dubbed a national war hero by slaying thousands of Israel's enemies, but still he has to wait for his appointed time to sit on the throne. Only after Saul is killed in battle is David finally crowned king.

Through all of David's narrow escapes from death and his agonizing wait to receive what God has promised him, David pens some of the most passionate words of Scripture. More than any other biblical writer, David extols the merciful character of God.

- "But I, by your great mercy, will come into your house; in reverence will I bow down toward your holy temple." (Psalm 5:7)

- "Surely goodness and mercy shall follow me all the days of my life: and I will dwell in the house of the LORD for ever." (Psalm 23:6 KJV)

- "Do not withhold your mercy from me, O LORD; may your love and your truth always protect me." (Psalm 40:11)

- "Answer me, O LORD, out of the goodness of your love; in your great mercy turn to me." (Psalm 69:16)

- "Do not hold against us the sins of the fathers; may your mercy come quickly to meet us, for we are in desperate need." (Psalm 79:8)

Time after time David pleads for God's mercy. This warrior king from humble pastures trusts in God's mercy. In his tumultuous years of waiting, David cries out for God's unmerited favor. We have much to learn from David's prayers and his unshakable belief in his merciful Creator.

Next time you're dogged by discouraging circumstances and grow tired of waiting, turn to the Psalms and emulate David's honest dialogue with a merciful God. Then flip to Luke 23. Scan down through the events of Jesus's crucifixion and stop at verses 39–43:

One of the criminals who hung there hurled insults at him: "Aren't you the Christ? Save yourself and us!"

But the other criminal rebuked him. "Don't you fear God," he said, "since you are under the same sentence? We are punished justly, for we are getting what our deeds deserve. But this man has done nothing wrong."

Then he said, "Jesus, remember me when you come into your kingdom."

Jesus answered him, "I tell you the truth, today you will be with me in paradise."

One of the convicted felons on a cross next to Christ vehemently attacks the Messiah's character. The other dying outlaw defends God's character. This condemned offender admits, "We are getting what our deeds deserve." In his final moments of life, this criminal fully understands that he deserves no mercy.

Yet a God rich in mercy hears the evildoer's last confession and guarantees a place for him in heaven. This merciful God did the same for you. Extending mercy was Jesus's last action just before he died.

God is no celestial Soup Nazi. He's got plenty of mercy and soup for you. No need to come back in one year. Come as you are, right now, and just hold out your hands. For as Augustine knew, "God gives where he finds empty hands."[5]

Writing in the Dirt
Your Understanding God

Understanding is the reward of faith.

Augustine of Hippo

Two days. Forty-eight hours. Nearly three thousand minutes. Sometimes two days zip by like a nanosecond, especially if the days are Saturday and Sunday. Other times the hour hand sputters, stalls, and schleps along, barely moving Father Time. I remember well the two longest days of my life.

On the blustery morning of March 10, 2001, I awake in

my childhood bedroom. Sixty miles away in critical care, my mother never opens her eyes.

Instead of dressing quickly to get back to the hospital, I can barely move. My jaw throbs. Muscle spasms contort the right side of my face. Viselike pain grips my neck. In an attempt to deaden the throbbing, I cram my face into the pillow.

A misaligned temporary crown proves to be the culprit of my facial pain. A restless night on a lumpy pillow aggravates the herniated discs in my neck. But what about the turmoil in my soul?

Tears cascade down my fevered cheeks as I stumble to the bathroom. My distressed mind and body revolt—I vomit four times in thirty minutes. Dizzy and weak, I collapse on the bed and sob to God, "Lord, have mercy! Help me. Stop my pain!"

Lacking the energy to dig through my luggage for my journal, I find a notepad and pen at the side of the bed. I scribble these desperate words: "I'm on the edge of hell, and the flames have scorched my soul."

I can almost feel hell's merciless flames as my family and I wait for Mom to succumb to death after her massive stroke. Dragging myself to the hospital that morning, little do I know how the hours will crawl during my second day at Mom's bedside. She lies motionless, hooked to a hodgepodge of tubes and monitors. The stroke she suffered earlier in the week basically short-circuited her brain stem, causing her body temperature to shoot up and cripple her organs.

I handle phone calls to the neurologist while Dad sits near Mom, staring blankly at the television in the corner. On the TV screen, fans rant for their team to win the boys' state basketball tournament. In contrast, my distraught father slumps in a chair, trapped in silent grief.

"Will she be able to recover from this?" I ask the neurologist. "Or is she already brain dead?" He delivers the grim news. Without the life support sustaining Mom's heart and lungs, she will soon die on her own. The doctor recommends that we gather the family and remove Mom from the ventilator. How to break this news to my dad and brothers and their wives is not something I learned in school.

At about 5:30 p.m. my parents' former pastor, now a hospital chaplain, leads our family in prayer and singing. The grandkids' tears are especially touching as we take turns saying our final good-byes to Mom.

After the nurses remove Mom from the ventilator, I ask one of them, "How long do you think she'll live now?" The kind woman reassures me, "Considering her condition, I would say about fifteen minutes."

Those fifteen minutes stretch into an hour. Nine of us huddle around Mom's bed, occasionally stroking her hand and face and whispering, "I love you . . . it's OK . . . you can go now." Another hour passes, then another. Her raspy breathing remains steady. A nurse drifts in every so often to check the blinking machines still recording Mom's vitals.

Another hour slips by, then another. So much for "fifteen minutes."

On one of my brief trips out of the room, I ask a nurse at the station desk, "How long can a patient hang on like this? I mean, have you seen other patients live this long after taking them off the ventilator?"

"Oh, sure," she replies matter-of-factly. "We had one guy live several days. We finally moved him to a rehab center, where he died."

I sigh and slowly shuffle back to Mom's room, wrestling with God.

Several days? Lord, no. Mom's ready to be with you. Please, take her soon.

"Soon" lasts another three hours. A little after two o'clock in the morning, Mom's fight ends—eight and a half hours after our beside farewell service. Our family signs a few administrative papers, then trudges down the critical-care hallway for the last time. Around three o'clock we enter the misty parking lot, chilled less by the bracing rain than by the icy fingers of finality.

At some point the death of a loved one will cause each of us to feel the chill of finality. Mary and Martha surely felt it as they paced near Lazarus's bedside, hoping their brother would recover, only to watch him die while Jesus tarried at the river. Waiting for a loved one to be healed or released from suffering is one of life's most exhausting tests of endurance. It's a wait that can make you feel like you're on the edge of hell with a scorched soul.

In his letter to the American people upon leaving office in 1989, President Ronald Reagan wrote, "I now begin the journey that will lead me into the sunset of my life."[1] For the next ten years, petite Nancy Reagan endearingly guarded the health of her larger-than-life husband while, day after day, Alzheimer's dimmed the once-great orator's mind. During that decade of persistence, tenderness, and love, Nancy Reagan rarely left the ailing Gipper's side.

On June 11, 2004, millions of people worldwide watched a fading California sunset spread across the sky at an emotional hilltop burial ceremony for America's beloved fortieth president. Who can forget those gripping last moments when Nancy pressed her face against Ronnie's casket and whispered, "I love you."

While this frail yet brave first lady gently patted and ran her slender hand across the polished coffin, many of us watching on television sobbed. For some of us the tears fell harder because we understand the wretched agony of saying a final farewell to our dearest loved ones.

Mary and Martha endured such a graveside parting without their close comrade Jesus at their side. Jesus's unexplained absence during their time of deepest sorrow must have ripped deeply into their already burdened hearts. Weary and weeping outside the burial cave, perhaps the sisters reassured each other in hushed voices: "Surely, Jesus will arrive any minute. He's not too far away. Surely, he wouldn't miss our last good-bye to Lazarus."

But Jesus did miss the somber service. He missed Lazarus's final breaths days earlier. Jesus was a no-show during this family's darkest hour.

Many of us wait and wait for God to meet us in our desperate moments, but sometimes it seems he arrives way after the time we felt we needed him most. We wonder if he really understands what we're facing. We cross-examine God: "Where are you? What part of 'I've had it with waiting' don't you understand? Do you really get it? Do you really get me?"

Knowing that someone "gets" us makes us feel listened to and understood. Unfortunately, we sometimes think of God as a slick-haired mafia don who hacks at us in a raspy voice, "I don't care what yooz think 'bout waitin'. Dooz as yooz told, and no onez gets a'hurt. Capiche?"

I asked one of my Italian-blooded friends for a translation of the Italian *capisci* (from which the more familiar slang *capiche* is derived) and learned that it means "you understand." The dictionary definition adds, "to grasp the meaning of . . . to be thoroughly familiar with the character and propensities of."[2]

I especially appreciate knowing that someone who understands me is "thoroughly familiar" with my "character and propensities." When it comes to waiting, sometimes my not-so-ravishing character and propensities ooze their way into my responses to situations and people.

This is when I'm glad I have God as my greatest ally. My *feeling* that he doesn't understand my circumstances or me does not alter the *fact* that he does understand.

Waiting is the ideal time to hunker down in God's Word to find out that he is not some celestial computer incapable of grasping the angst of humans in wait mode, but rather an in-touch God who "gets" us.

In my quest to see if God is understanding, I discovered some intriguing Bible passages: "To God belong wisdom and power; counsel and understanding are his," declared Job, weary from waiting for his grief and physical misery to end (Job 12:13). King David extolled God's limitless understanding when he wrote, "Give thanks to the LORD of lords . . . who by his understanding made the heavens, his love endures forever (Psalm 136:3, 5) and, "Great is our Lord and mighty in power; his understanding has no limit" (Psalm 147:5).

King David's son Solomon shared his own wise words about God's understanding nature: "The LORD gives wisdom, and from his mouth come knowledge and understanding" (Proverbs 2:6). "By wisdom the LORD laid the earth's foundations, by understanding he set the heavens in place" (Proverbs 3:19).

And we can't forget the prophet Isaiah when it comes to documenting God's comprehension in designing and caring for the universe: "Whom did the LORD consult to enlighten him, and who taught him the right way? Who was it that taught him knowledge or showed him the path of understanding? . . . Do you not know? Have you not heard? The LORD is the everlasting God, the Creator of the ends of the earth. He will not grow tired or weary, and his understanding no one can fathom" (Isaiah 40:14, 28).

God understands how every atom fits together, so why would he need our help in making sure everything stays synchronized on our little timetables? Maybe we can't fully fathom God's understanding, but can we comprehend that he does understand us—particularly when life is putting us off? Are we willing to at least entertain the possibility that God grasps the intimate details of our struggle with waiting? That he has a clear picture of the emotional storm that batters us as we hold on for the "overdue" answers to our prayers?

If only we humans were better at extending God's understanding ways to others as they wait. If only we were as perceptive as the Rabbit and the Skin Horse in the classic tale *The Velveteen Rabbit*. Perhaps you recall the Skin Horse's memorable explanation to the Rabbit of how playthings become Real. "Generally, by the time you are Real, most of your hair has been loved off, and your eyes drop out and you get loose in the joints and very shabby," the Skin Horse says. "But these things don't matter at all, because once you are Real you can't be ugly, except to people who don't understand."[3]

> WAITING IS DIFFICULT ENOUGH WITHOUT THE PRESSURE AND BURDEN OF DEALING WITH PEOPLE WHO CAN'T IDENTIFY WITH YOU.

Waiting can make us a little loose in the joints and shabby; so can people who don't understand. Waiting is difficult enough without the pressure and burden of dealing with people who can't identify with you.

In June 2000 a high-school student in the tiny Russian village of Vorobyovo discovered this firsthand. Russian President Vladimir Putin didn't "get it" when six graduating students wrote to the Kremlin. Seventeen-year-old Anya Provorova and her classmates wanted a video camera to record their graduation. They decided to send a request for help straight to their national leader. Surely it couldn't hurt to ask.

Nobody remembers who came up with the idea to write to Putin, and nobody signed the letter. Realistically, the students didn't think the unsigned letter would even be delivered. But on June 8 two government inspectors visited the tiny school. The missive had made it to Putin's desk, and he was not amused.

Apparently the salutation to "The Esteemed Vladimir Vladimirovich Putin" lacked an exclamation point at the end of the phrase. (Personally, I'd be thrilled that the students had correctly spelled that middle name!) And to top it off, the letter referred to the president using the Russian word for *you* without capitalizing it. A missing exclamation point and lowercased *you* proved to be a major no-no in Moscow.

The inspectors interrogated the Vorobyovo students and determined that Anya's handwriting matched the letter's penmanship. Although the simple request for a video camera was a group effort, young Anya paid dearly for the punctuation errors.

A week later, on her graduation day, Anya learned that an administrative fiat had lowered her final grades and stripped away the silver medal she'd expected. With her graduation honors ruined, instead of heading proudly to medical school, Anya dejectedly enrolled in a dairy academy. Instead of healing people, Anya would be herding cows. All because of two innocent punctuation blunders and a leader who didn't understand.[4]

Now, lest you want to impeach President Putin, remember that we all botch up at times. Mistakes and misunderstandings are as old as earth's inaugural family. In history's first sibling rivalry, Cain killed his younger brother Abel over a hunk of animal fat (Genesis 4:1–8). The world's first murder was not in a dank back alley but on the open fields of Eden. Perhaps Cain didn't have the patience to gather a more acceptable offering for God, so he chucked waiting and opted for drastic measures. Maybe Cain just didn't take the time to understand.

A few centuries later a distant relative of earth's first brothers didn't take the time to understand either. In the book of Jonah we read that Jonah receives instructions straight from God to warn the Assyrian people in the capital city of Nineveh to change their sinful ways or face judgment. But Jonah doesn't wait around to obey his understanding God. He doesn't care to acknowledge the rebels of Nineveh. He certainly isn't going to prepare and present sermons to these cruel Assyrians. Instead, he hits the beach running.

Jonah's understanding of the Assyrians doesn't match up with God's compassionate view of these pagan people. Impatient with God's plan, Jonah decides to hop on a ship and sail northeast to Tarshish, on the southern tip of Spain. Or "as far away from GOD as he could get," says Jonah 1:3 in the *The Message.* We'll follow this Bible version to track Jonah's adventurous escape.

There's nothing like relaxing on a Mediterranean cruise thousands of miles from home to help one escape life's challenges. Napping in the hold of the ship, and probably dreaming of his R&R plans at a Spanish villa, Jonah is rudely awakened by the ship's captain. Towering waves pound the wooden vessel, and it is about to splinter.

Panicked, the sailors send up desperate prayers to their gods. But the captain seeks out Jonah and demands: "Get up! Pray to your god! Maybe your god will see we're in trouble and rescue us" (Jonah 1:6).

Under pressure from the sailors, Jonah admits that he is running from God and advises them to throw him overboard. As the storm rages more violently, the men finally heave the runaway into the tumultuous waves. The squall stops, and God directs a whale of a fish to swallow Jonah.

The complimentary three-day and three-night stay in the fish's belly isn't exactly an exotic seaside vacation. Jonah sloshes around for some seventy hours in the fish's stomach acid. Ensnared in the fish's belly,

Jonah finally realizes it's time to take hold of a spiritual anchor. We find his prayer in Jonah 2:6–7: "I was as far down as a body can go, and the gates were slamming shut behind me forever—yet you pulled me up from that grave alive, O GOD, my God! When my life was slipping away, I remembered GOD, and my prayer got through to you, made it all the way to your Holy Temple."

In your waiting, you may feel "as far down as a body can go." Tense shoulders, headaches, and stomach knots can assail your body when you're tangled in red tape. Postponements and deferred solutions can drown your faith in God when you doubt that he comprehends your plight. But when you're floundering on the high seas of waiting, it's not the time to abandon ship—or your confidence in a God who "stretched out the heavens by his understanding" (Jeremiah 10:12).

> ENSNARED IN THE FISH'S BELLY, JONAH FINALLY REALIZES IT'S TIME TO TAKE HOLD OF A SPIRITUAL ANCHOR.

After Jonah's unpleasant bonding with the marine animal, you'd think he would tune in for good to God's plans. Jonah did eventually show up in Nineveh, and he warned the inhabitants to repent. But when the people show remorse for their sinful ways and God relents from punishing them, Jonah throws a fit. Infuriated Jonah prays, "So, GOD, if you won't kill them, kill *me*! I'm better off dead!" (Jonah 4:3).

Jonah pouts alone east of town. When the blistering heat and winds arise, the compassionate and understanding Creator appoints a shady plant to comfort the grumpy prophet. The book of Jonah ends with us wondering if the clueless Jonah ever really understood that God chose to spare "this big city of more than a hundred and twenty thousand childlike people who don't yet know right from wrong" (Jonah 4:11).

Jonah's story speaks volumes about our God who comprehends, who truly understands, that many of us childish people mix up right and wrong. God always catches the intricacies of our daily lives. He takes in and grasps our purpose every second we walk on this earth. God totally "gets" us!

A friend sent me a story by an unknown author about a church struggling with ascertaining God's intentions for his followers. One Sunday morning an old cowboy visits a sizable church in an affluent part of the city. Although the wrangler's denim shirt, jeans, and boots are impeccably clean, they are noticeably tattered and worn.

Carrying a somewhat shabby hat and dog-eared Bible, the cowboy moseys in and sits down. All the well-heeled people seated near him scoot away. No one deigns to look at or speak to the stranger. Everyone is appalled by the audacity of this man to wear such casual attire to church.

The pastor pontificates about the horrors of hell and lectures about the money the congregation fails to give to accomplish God's work. As the cowboy leaves the service, the pastor intercepts him and says firmly, "Before you come back, have a talk with God and ask him what he thinks would be appropriate attire to worship here."

The horseman promises to oblige and the next week shows up at the church wearing the same clean-but-ragged outfit. Again people turn up their noses. At the close of the service, the pastor marches up to the cowboy and sternly asserts: "I thought I asked you to speak to God before you came back to our church."

"I did," the old broncobuster calmly replies.

"Well, what did he tell you the proper attire should be for worshiping here?"

"Well, sir," the kindly cowboy explains, "God told me that he didn't have a clue what I should wear. He said he'd never been here before."

I chuckle at this humorous story. But I appreciate that in reality, our God always has a clue. God knows our every thought and intention—even the motives of those who profess him with their lips but whose actions point to a lifeless faith. Even people like those in the fictionalized church, and even people from the religious community of Jesus's day.

If you've seen any of the compelling Gospel-based movies such as *JESUS*, *The Gospel of John*, and *The Passion of the Christ*, you may recall the poignant scene from John 8:1–11. Jesus leads an early-morning Scripture lesson at the temple courts in Jerusalem.

With the crowds gathered and intent on hearing the Messiah, the teachers of the Law and the Pharisees drag a frightened woman before the group. The religious nobility force this humiliated woman to her feet before the judging crowd.

The holier-than-thou authorities snarl, "Teacher, this woman was caught in the act of adultery. In the Law Moses commanded us to stone such women. Now what do you say?" (John 8:4–5).

Before we find out Jesus's response to these accusers, let's take a minute to glance over the plaintiffs' dossiers. The Pharisees were one of three Jewish sects (along with the Sadducees and Essenes) at the time of this first-century encounter. The Pharisees were a religious faction as well as a political party. These pious politicians and students of the Law served as watchdogs of the Torah and Talmud—they subscribed to a complex system of oral laws and tradition to direct faithful Jews in obedience to God's commandments.

Many people today view the Pharisees as elitist hypocrites who smacked wooden rulers across the knuckles of weaker Jews. Let's just say these devout reformers were not known for kissing babies and handing out loaves and fish.

But keep in mind that one well-respected Pharisee showed the better side of some in the infamous group. Nicodemus, who at first didn't comprehend the truth of Christ's claim that people must be born again (John 3:1–21), later defended the Son of God.

At the end of John 7, we read how Nicodemus risks his reputation with his fellow members of the ruling council the day before the Pharisees dump the adulterous woman at Jesus's feet. Jesus addresses the temple crowds, who remain divided over their belief in him.

> GOD ALWAYS HAS A CLUE. GOD KNOWS OUR EVERY THOUGHT AND INTENTION.

The temple guards and Pharisees break into a heated discussion about this rabble-rouser from Nazareth. Some want to seize Jesus and arrest him.

Gutsy Nicodemus interrupts, "Does our law condemn anyone without first hearing him to find out what he is doing?" (John 7:51). Immediately Nicodemus's comrades cut him off, asserting that no prophet—Jesus in particular—can come from Nicodemus's homeland of Galilee. The encounter ends abruptly, and everyone heads home.

But at dawn the next day, Jesus is back teaching the crowds. This time the religious leaders decide to up the ante and test this rabbi who speaks of being sent by God and claims to offer "living water." The devout Jews force the adulterous woman to stand before Jesus, hoping to trap him into contradicting the Law.

Jesus's response is one of my favorite scenes in Scripture. "Jesus bent down and started to write on the ground with his finger" (John 8:6). The great teacher nonchalantly stoops to doodle in the dirt with his finger. I wish the Bible told us what he wrote in the Judean soil. Maybe he drew a smiley face, maybe a peace sign. Maybe he practiced his signature in Hebrew.

One thing is certain: Jesus's casual response only provokes the Pharisees to badger him more about the woman's moral misstep. We can almost hear them sneer, "She's a whore! She's a slut! Our laws demand that she be stoned for two-timing her husband."

Eventually Jesus pauses from his finger drawing and stands up. "If any one of you is without sin, let him be the first to throw a stone at her," he calmly pronounces before stooping back to the ground to continue his writing (John 8:7).

> "At this, those who heard began to go away one at a time, the older ones first, until only Jesus was left, with the woman still standing there. Jesus straightened up and asked her, "Woman, where are they? Has no one condemned you?"
>
> "No one, sir," she said.
>
> "Then neither do I condemn you," Jesus declared. "Go now and leave your life of sin." (John 8:9–11)

Wow! Isn't it amazing what a little understanding can do? Jesus understands what led this woman to seek the arms of another man. He understands why the Pharisees paraded her into the temple. Jesus understands both the woman's shame and the mob's blame.

Jesus understands every sin in this woman's life. He understands every sin in her accusers' lives. Jesus understands that we all deserve punishment for our sins; that's why he came to earth to take our punishment on himself: "Christ died for sins once for all, the righteous for the unrighteous, to bring you to God" (1 Peter 3:18).

God sympathizes with us and draws us to himself. Because Jesus comprehends the adulterous woman's real needs, he releases her from moral condemnation into spiritual freedom. Yet his actions that day seem to affect more than one life.

Perhaps Nicodemus left the courtyard further convinced that this Galilean teacher could deliver on his promise that "whoever believes in him shall not perish but have eternal life" (John 3:16). For not long after Jesus's showdown with the Pharisees, after Jesus is crucified, Nicodemus risks his noble religious status by lugging seventy-five pounds of fragrant perfumes to preserve Jesus's body before burial. Nicodemus helps Joseph of Arimathea carefully wrap the fallen Savior's body, and together they carry him to a stone tomb (John 19:39–42). They place Jesus in a rock dugout much like the one used for Lazarus.

Braving the ridicule and retaliation of his fellow Pharisees, Nicodemus honors Jesus with a final farewell. Not before the grieving masses, but simply with a friend in a garden cemetery before the sunlight turns to darkness.

The Bible never mentions Nicodemus again, so we don't know for certain what he finally decided about Jesus the Messiah. But we face our own decision of faith. Are we willing to accept that Jesus didn't just write in the dirt that day? Jesus was waiting. He was waiting for the right time to show that he always understands.

Capiche?

Breathe Deep

Your Patient God

Never think that God's delays are God's denials.
Hold on; hold fast; hold out. Patience is genius.

Georges-Louis Leclerc Buffon

Chanting mantras while sitting for nine days without water, food, or sleep pushes Genshin Fujinami to the edge of collapse. Yet this *doiri*, or "entering the temple," trial is only a small part of the regimen the Buddhist priest undertakes for seven years while pursuing the "path to enlightenment." The ritual, which dates back to the eighth century, requires the devoted to complete a grueling spiritual journey while climbing alone the five peaks of the Hiei Mountains above the ancient capital of Kyoto, Japan.

Numerous "marathon monks" of the Tendai sect have attempted this quest. Since 1885 only forty-six have returned alive. According to tradition, any monk, or *gyoja*, who cannot endure to the finish must kill himself by hanging or disemboweling.

Genshin vows not to let this be his fate. Wearing a handmade white robe and flimsy straw sandals, Genshin leaves the Enryakuji Hoshuin Temple, southwest of Tokyo, Japan, in 1996. He plods mile after mile along the arduous course and faces numerous iron-man challenges along the way. During each of the first three years, the determined monk rises at midnight for one hundred consecutive days to run along an eighteen-mile trail around Mount Hiei—stopping to pray 250 times. His only companions: candles, a prayer book, and a sack of vegetarian food.

In each of the next two years, Genshin makes these difficult runs on two hundred days straight. In the winters he takes a break to do temple chores. In the fifth year he also faces the nine days of chanting and fasting. The next year he walks 37.5 miles every day for one hundred days.

In the seventh year Genshin hikes 52.5 miles for one hundred days and then eighteen miles for another hundred days before returning to his home temple. When the forty-four-year-old monk completes his trek in September 2003, he has covered 24,800 miles, a distance almost equivalent to a trip around the globe—every step in thin straw sandals.[1]

Can you imagine taking on this herculean challenge? Can you imagine enduring all those miles without your favorite hiking boots or walking shoes? My feet ache just thinking about this marathon monk's feat. I've climbed four of Colorado's fourteen-thousand-foot mountains, all in back-to-back Saturdays, but I had appropriate gear and fun snacks. Even though I don't endorse Genshin's religion, he's still a noble model of endurance and patience to me.

I'm nowhere close to having Genshin's patience. I used to consider myself a fairly patient person until I started working on this chapter. Even now, as I type, I'm getting a bit antsy. Last week I learned that I have a separated shoulder with partially torn ligaments, an inflamed tendon, and bone spurs. I'm now wearing a contraption that looks like a straitjacket with arm slots. What fun!

What's even more delightful is when my physical therapist tries to move my arm and shoulder to increase my range of motion. The other day I screamed like a frantic orangutan when one exercise accidentally jammed my collarbone into my shoulder blade.

I admit, I am not a patient patient. I also must confess that it's my impatience that landed me in this predicament. If only I hadn't tried to increase the weights in my workout too quickly. If only I hadn't stubbornly wielded a crowbar during that demolition project. If only I had waited for help instead of trying to lift some heavy items in the garage by myself.

My impatience has caught up with me—painfully. Now I'm forced to be patient as I wade through the morass of appointments, tests, insurance forms, and therapy sessions. I'm also waiting three more weeks to see an orthopedic surgeon who specializes in shoulders. How long, how long, O Lord, before I can use my arm again?

A minimum of six to eight weeks, they say. Healing takes time, they say. Alas, try as I might, I cannot speed up the healing process.

Believe me, working as a one-armed writer is sure to teach one patience. Now that I can't accomplish my normal, lengthy to-do list (lawn mowing is definitely out . . . oh darn!), I'm slowing down to contemplate the essence of patience. Gradually I'm learning to lean into waiting and embrace the lessons of patience it produces.

Patience essentially means enduring trials and pains calmly and without grumbling. Being patient means not being hasty, impetuous, or impulsive. A patient person remains cool instead of getting hotheaded when the heat is on. I wish I had responded with that kind of serene, even temper one morning in the Congo's bush country.

> WHEN A FIFTEEN-FOOT BOA CONSTRICTOR STRANGLED A GOAT NEXT TO OUR OPEN-DOOR HUT, I REACHED NEW HEIGHTS OF FORBEARANCE.

Dragging oneself through weeks with no electricity, running water, or indoor toilets can send one over the edge. So can a daily diet of canned sardines and rice. Not to mention living in cramped mud huts, taking cold cup baths, and battling a bout of malaria.

Yet all those inconveniences were minor compared with the excitement and honor of showing the *JESUS* film to countless Africans in remote villages and jungle communities in Zaire (now the Democratic Republic of the Congo). I loved serving as a chaperone to sixteen American college students on this two-month mission adventure.

I smiled my way through our continual tests of unusual foods and exotic sights. (I literally could not stomach eating monkey, and when a fifteen-foot boa constrictor strangled a goat next to our open-door hut, I reached new heights of forbearance.)

Barbara Kingsolver's best-selling novel *The Poisonwood Bible* is replete with intriguing descriptions of the Congo. Here are a couple of my favorites:

The jungle closed us out with its great green wall of trees, bird calls, animal breathing, all as permanent as a heartbeat we heard in our sleep. Surrounding us was a thick, wet, living stand of trees and tall grasses stretching all the way across Congo. And we were nothing but little mice squirming through it in our dark little pathways. In Congo, it seems the land owns the people.[2]

Congo sprawls on the middle of the world. Sun rises, sun sets, six o'clock exactly. Everything that comes of morning undoes itself before nightfall: rooster walks back into forest, fires die down, birds coo-coo, sun sinks away, sky bleeds, passes out, goes dark, nothing exists. Ashes to ashes.[3]

After a week in a remote region northwest of the capital city Kinshasa, where the sky does indeed seem to bleed and pass out, our four-member team eagerly awaited our return to civilization. Put on some safari background music as I relive this adventure for you.

Our team is assured that a truck will pick us up at 8:00 a.m. and take us to Kitwit, where we will catch a bus back to Kinshasa. (Kitwit is the epicenter of the dreaded Ebola outbreak in 1995. Fortunately, we visited this village a dozen years before Ebola did.)

I am still feeling wiped out after my bout with malaria, and I've been out of bed only one day before our travel day. The thought of city life— even a city fuming with acrid pollution and political chaos—sure increases my waning stamina. My bags are packed, and I am raring to go at seven o'clock that June morning. Our Zairian pastor friend will accompany us on our journey. We wait and listen for the roar of an engine to slice through the cavernous jungle. We wait for hours and hours.

With no telephones or e-mail, we must wait for someone to deliver a message in person. About noon we learn that our truck needs a tire repaired. We are told our ride will arrive by three o'clock.

More waiting. Finally, about seven that evening—eleven hours behind schedule—the green, military-style truck rumbles onto the missionary compound. We bid fond farewells to our host family and clamber into the back of the vehicle, already jammed with a dozen Zairians with their baskets and chickens.

Onward into the dense, shadowy trees we venture. Two hours into our bone-jarring journey, the massive truck lurches to a stop. The driver barks orders for all of us to bail out so he can maneuver the truck over a muddy stream.

There's nothing like crawling in a straight skirt over the side of a truck five feet above ground . . . in a jungle alive with the screeching of countless nearby animals . . . in the dark. At that moment I long for trendy, safari-style khakis and thick-soled boots. I long for my own bed, where being dumped out into a black-on-black forest deep in the Congo would be just a dream.

Keep in mind, I am still recovering from a mosquito-borne illness, and I waited half a day for this dilapidated hunk of metal. You haven't lived until you've climbed out of a behemoth truck into the soggy soil of a tropical jungle engulfed by a cacophony of *wooooo-hhhhaaaa-hee-hee-heekkkk* sounds of the night.

Next, we inch across the stream, balancing on a couple of slippery bamboo poles serving as a makeshift bridge. Then, one by one, we hitch up our bloomers and wriggle up the side of the truck to settle down for the rest of our moonlit excursion.

By the time we drive into Kitwit, it is nearly midnight. My entire body aches as we again hurl ourselves over the side of the truck to set foot on dry ground. With no streetlights to guide us, we four Americans huddle around our Zairian pastor. We give him some money, and he walks across the street to a thatch-roofed "bus terminal" to buy our tickets to Kinshasa. Exhausted and a bit bruised from our Congo convoy, I thank God that we survived without being attacked by a ravenous lion or wildebeest.

A few minutes later the pastor returns and tells us that we will need to wait until 5:00 a.m. or later to get tickets. So we plop our backpacks and duffel bags in the dirt and collapse on top of them. Nodding off into fitful sleep, we are jolted awake around three in the morning by a group of young Zairian men bolting out of the shadows.

These eager locals line up next to the ticket hut, and our pastor friend scurries over to them. Part of business in this poor village is to sell your spot in line to someone waiting for a bus ticket. Our friend wants to ensure that we Americans would get seats on that day's bus to the capital, so he pays the young hustlers to guarantee our spots in line.

At this point we all give up trying to sleep and just sit in the damp darkness waiting for our bus. Fortunately, the old vehicle that looks like a cross between a school bus and a railroad car snarls to life at 7:00 a.m.

Exhausted, sore, and famished, I let the students board ahead of me. Just as I lift my backpack into the stairwell of the bus, a Zairian woman wedges her lithe body in front of me. With a chicken under one arm and a bag strapped on the other, the twenty-something woman shoves herself and her bulky belongings between the bus driver and me.

Stunned and nearly tumbling backward, I can't believe this woman's rudeness. She seems panicked about finding a seat. Her forceful jostling sparks instinctive fear in me. *Oh no, what if she takes the last seat, and I'm marooned in this desolate outback for several more days!*

I lightly poke my elbow into her back and stammer for words she'd understand. This is Francophone Africa, and I only know *un peu*

French, such as *je m'appelle* and *la salle de bains*. So pardon my French, but I shout at her, "*Excusez vous!*" Not *excusez moi*, but excuse YOU!

It's fortunate that I don't know any French or Lingali swear words, or I might hurl them her way. I want to scream, "Out of my way-y-y-y," as we twist in a luggage gridlock. I am definitely bigger than she is, but she has a beady-eyed chicken under her arm and the vexing look of a disgruntled witch doctor.

German philosopher Friedrich Nietzsche once said, "A sure way to irritate people and to put evil thoughts into their heads is to keep them waiting a long time. This makes them immoral."[4]

At that moment in that dusty Congolese village, all vestiges of patience drain from my being, and I dance on the edge of immorality. But just as quickly as evil thoughts line up like wallflowers in my head, I sense God's calming spirit. I choose to let this stranger board ahead of me, even if it means I'll be abandoned to another miserable day of waiting.

In the previous twenty-four hours I had been stretched to my limit. I had waited for a broken-down truck that tossed me around in a perilous jungle ride, finally depositing me in a sparse village in utter darkness. Then I'd waited on the street all night for a seat on an ancient bus, only to have my trip to civilization threatened by a pushy, poultry-toting stranger. Thankfully, God saved me a seat that morning, and more importantly, he increased my understanding that waiting refines in us the character of patience. Bit by bit, waiting for people to show up, waiting when we're literally sick and tired, and waiting when we're pushed outside our comfort zone can sand off our edginess.

Patience is a virtue that has been much written about over the ages. It seems many noteworthy citizens have pontificated on the immense value of patience. Famed painter Michelangelo stated, "Genius is eternal patience."[5] Renaissance author and father of deductive reasoning Francis Bacon said, "Who ever is out of patience is out of possession of their soul."[6] Nineteenth-century theologian Horace Bushnell believed, "The greatest and sublimest power is often simple patience."[7]

Simple patience. Is there such a thing? I, who am notoriously impatient for my fingernail polish to dry, wonder if I will ever be patient waiting for God to act on my behalf. Smudging my nail polish because of impatience is one thing; smearing my belief in God is quite another.

Perhaps you can relate. What trips you up when it comes to staying calm and sensible? What leaves you bursting to shout, "Out of my way"? What are the tiny grains of irritating sand that accumulate in your shoe and force you into a march of impatience?

> WHAT ARE THE TINY GRAINS OF IRRITATING SAND THAT ACCUMULATE IN YOUR SHOE AND FORCE YOU INTO A MARCH OF IMPATIENCE?

Be honest. At least your foibles and failures aren't recorded in this book or, worse yet, in the Bible. Oh, what the children of Israel might have done differently if they had known their restless and irritated reactions to waiting would be public record for all the world's generations to follow.

I highlight their intolerance for delay in these pages knowing that I might have made the same choices walking forty years in their sandals. I, who have to strap myself into a shoulder brace every morning. I, who nearly decked an African woman while on a mission trip.

"Perhaps there is only one cardinal sin: impatience," noted poet W. H. Auden. "Because of impatience we were driven out of Paradise, because of impatience we cannot return."[8] In the book of Exodus we read about the descendants of Adam and Eve, history's first impatient people, whose impetuousness barred them forever from paradise. Eve's itchy fingers clutched that forbidden fruit, and Adam just couldn't wait to join in. Because of their haste to fulfill their own desires, impatience is entwined in the DNA of every one of us.

Three-fourths of Exodus 15 is devoted to Moses and the children of Israel singing praise to God for rescuing them from Pharaoh and the Egyptian army. Exuberant and literally dancing before God, they belt out: "The LORD is my strength and my song; he has become my salvation. He is my God, and I will praise him" (Exodus 15:2). "Who among the gods is like you, O LORD? Who is like you—majestic in holiness, awesome in glory, working wonders?" (Exodus 15:11). "The LORD will reign for ever and ever" (Exodus 15:18).

After Miriam wraps up the hallelujah chorus, we see in verse 22 that Moses leads the people from the Red Sea into the wilderness. After three days of trekking in the hot wasteland, the Israelites are parched and desperate to refill their canteens and camels. But they find only bitter waters at Marah.

With no convenience store or babbling brook in sight, the Israelites "grumbled against Moses, saying, 'What are we to drink?'" (Exodus 15:24). *Grumbled* is the operative word here. The people didn't just curiously ask or politely inquire. They growl, roar, and hiss. Remember, patience essentially means to walk through tough circumstances calmly and without grumbling. Yeah, I know, that last part often trips me up too.

Three days earlier these nomads had victoriously celebrated the majesty of their Redeemer. How quickly they lift their walking sticks in defiance to the God who, it seems to them, has left them high and dry. Does that ever sound like us? We praise God joyously one minute and question his plans the next.

As we read over the last verses of Exodus 15, it's essential to note how

God responds to this water crisis. He practices patience. God listens to Moses's cry and then calmly directs him to toss a chuck of wood into the waters to sweeten them for drinking. But that isn't all. God then escorts his people to Elim, an oasis of twelve springs of water and seventy palms. Ahhhhh . . . in the soothing shade, sipping tumblers of fresh water and nibbling on delectable dates, the Israelites can finally cool their heels.

So what is God's purpose in making the Israelites wait for their needs to be supplied? Verse 25 tells us simply, "he tested them." When we wait, God tests our faith in his character and in his ability to provide what we truly need. He aligns obstacles in our paths as a means of analyzing our beliefs or diagnosing weak spots in our faith. Will we trust him, or will we focus on the unfavorable conditions we see and believe only the erratic emotions we feel?

Israel's grumbling at Marah is just the first of their myriad impatient moments with God in the wilderness. Two verses after we read about Moses and the gang resting at the oasis, we find them grumbling about food in the Desert of Sin. (With a geographic name like that, it must be a place that brings out the worst in people.)

The Israelites whine to Moses and Aaron, "If only we had died by the LORD's hand in Egypt! There we sat around pots of meat and ate all the food we wanted, but you have brought us out into this desert to starve this entire assembly to death" (Exodus 16:3).

I imagine the Israelite slaves, after lugging bricks all day, kicking back around an all-you-can-eat fondue fest. They dipped their fresh bread in meaty pots and toasted Pharaoh even if they didn't like his labor laws. If only they could return to Egypt with its savory aromas and rich culinary delights. Instead, they are forced to eat unleavened bread cakes (Exodus 12:39). For a while they live on leftovers.

But God again exercises patience and sweet reason: he quickly satisfies the hunger pangs of his children by providing manna and quail in abundance (Exodus 16:13–15). Moses assures the people, "You will know that it was the LORD when he gives you meat to eat in the evening and all the bread you want in the morning, because he has heard your grumbling against him. Who are we? You are not grumbling against us, but against the LORD" (Exodus 16:8).

Like the ancient Israelites, when you and I are grouchy and complain about waiting, we're not just carping about our circumstances; we are criticizing our Maker. Ouch! Outwardly we may appear serene, but inwardly we stew with impatience toward God.

> WHEN YOU AND I ARE GROUCHY AND COMPLAIN ABOUT WAITING, WE'RE NOT JUST CARPING ABOUT OUR CIRCUMSTANCES; WE ARE CRITICIZING OUR MAKER.

Solomon said, in Proverbs 19:11, "A man's wisdom gives him patience; it is to his glory to overlook an offense." God models for us an example of wise patience that overlooks offenses. He demonstrates his steadfast, controlled nature again when, as we see in Exodus 17, Israel runs into another water shortage. "They grumbled against Moses. They said, 'Why did you bring us up out of Egypt to make us and our children and livestock die of thirst?'" (Exodus 17:3).

This time the Israelites add their livestock to the weight of their complaint against God. Why, why did you deliver us from our oppressive enemies to let us all—even our flocks—shrivel up from thirst? They "grumbled against Moses," but God was their ultimate target. Yet instead of retaliating with a curt response or punitive action, God displays his long-suffering nature and again supplies plenty of refreshing H_2O.

If we continued on through Scripture, we'd find dozens of instances where God keeps his cool in the face of major meltdowns by his people. In Nehemiah 9 we read the Israelites' recounting of the mighty ways God provided for their ancestors through the centuries. In verses 15–17 these descendants of the Israelites in Moses's day specifically recall:

In their hunger you gave them bread from heaven and in their thirst you brought them water from the rock; you told them to go in and take possession of the land you had sworn with uplifted hand to give them.

But they, our forefathers, became arrogant and stiff-necked, and did not obey your commands. They refused to listen and failed to remember the miracles you performed among them. They became stiff-necked and in their rebellion appointed a leader in order to return to their slavery. But you are a forgiving God, gracious and compassionate, slow to anger and abounding in love. Therefore you did not desert them.

I love how *The Message* renders verse 17: "You, a forgiving God, gracious and compassionate, incredibly patient, with tons of love—you didn't dump them." God is incredibly patient and doesn't dump us, even when we are impatient. I'm continually amazed at how God serenely handles his worked-up kids.

In Nehemiah 9:30 the people add, "For many years you were patient with them." Bingo! Notice how verse 17 describes God as "slow to anger." This phrase appears frequently in the Bible and means that God is not hasty to react or quickly annoyed. He excels at waiting when the pressure mounts.

In Numbers 14:18 Moses says: "The LORD is slow to anger, abounding in love and forgiving sin and rebellion." The Psalms repeat the "slow to anger" theme at least three times (86:15; 103:8; 145:8).

The prophets Joel, Jonah, and Nahum pick the same words in their writings.

Joel explains, "God is kind and merciful. He takes a deep breath, puts up with a lot, this most patient God, extravagant in love, always ready to cancel catastrophe" (Joel 2:13 MSG). I don't know about you, but I just know God takes plenty of deep breaths over me. My "most patient God" puts up with a lot from his daughter named Beth Joy.

God himself proclaims that he is "slow to anger" (Exodus 34:6). One of my mom's favorite lines was, "I'm not bragging or complaining, I'm just stating a fact." God is not bragging; he's simply stating a fact: I, the Lord, am patient.

In the delightful movie *The Terminal*, viewers follow the predicament of Viktor Navorski (Tom Hanks), who flies into New York's John F. Kennedy International Airport from his fictitious country of Krakhozia. Ready to pass through customs and savor the Big Apple, Viktor learns his Eastern European homeland has erupted in civil war. Airport authorities deny Viktor access to the United States. Yet until Krakhozia settles its hostilities, Viktor cannot return home. He is essentially a man without a country.

The Terminal is loosely based on the real-life dilemma of a passenger expelled from Iran who then faced a bureaucratic snafu at the Charles DeGaulle Airport outside Paris. Once the traveler was cleared, he refused to leave. I've spent too many hours waiting in airports to refuse to leave one. Airports are a test of patience.

In the movie, whose promotional tagline is "Life is waiting," Viktor schleps his battered brown suitcase around the airport while he waits. He peers at television monitors throughout the terminal and waits for good news from home. Viktor waits for the American authorities to stamp his passport to freedom. He settles into an out-of-use gate at the airport, making a hard bed out of those unforgiving plastic seats. He waits every day for his passport to be approved so he can walk out the doors of JFK.

At one point Viktor is living on free crackers and condiments from the airport's fast-food stops. He creatively layers saltines with ketchup and mustard to make a mini carbo sandwich. Not exactly manna and quail, but at least we never hear Viktor grumble at God.

In fact, this polite traveler from abroad smiles throughout his prolonged ordeal in JFK and patiently remarks, "I v-v-vait." For months and months Viktor vaits—er, waits—as countless people nonchalantly zip in and out of the airport with ease. In case you haven't seen this lighthearted movie, I won't spoil the ending for you; but let's just say Viktor is a patient fellow.

So was Thomas Edison. The master scientist failed two thousand times before he invented the light bulb. When a reporter asked Edison about how it felt to come up short again and again, the scientific genius replied, "I never failed once. It just happened to be a two thousand-step process."[9]

Edison patented 1,093 inventions in his eighty-four years, and every one of them required skilled steadfastness and patience. But as enduring and persistent as the brilliant Thomas Edison was, he could never outshine God's patience. Neither can I; neither can you.

As much as we squirm and grumble when our lives seem to stall, we can learn—bit by bit—to embrace patience in our everyday moments of waiting. God is our mentor in how to breathe deeply and count to ten.

In the Gospels, Jesus shows tremendous forbearance during the darkest hours of his life. Knowing that he will soon face merciless beatings and a cruel death, Jesus takes his three closest disciples into the Garden of Gethsemane. Jesus asks Peter, James, and John to pray as he slips away to a nearby spot to agonize in prayer himself.

Three times Jesus returns to find his comrades slumbering instead of praying. In his time of desperate need, the Son of Man asks his close companions to support him in prayer. Instead, the disciples choose to get some shuteye.

If I were Jesus, I'd be crushed or irritated. But the Messiah doesn't get defensive or rude. He calmly encourages the men: "Pray so that you will not fall into temptation" (Luke 22:46). In some of his final minutes with his beloved friends, Jesus is evenhanded and composed.

He remains unruffled even as the bloodthirsty mob wielding swords and clubs troop into the garden. The traitor, Judas, and the religious leaders' thugs press in to drag Jesus away. In a frenzied burst of panic, Peter grabs his sword and whacks off the right ear of the high priest's servant.

John is the only one to record this maimed servant's name—Malchus (John 18:10). Physician Luke is the only one to record what Jesus does as soon as he sees the blood pouring from Malchus's head. "Jesus answered, 'No more of this!' And he touched the man's ear and healed him" (Luke 22:51).

In those seconds of surprise and terror, Peter impatiently lifts his hand to lash out. Jesus patiently lifts his hand to restore and heal.

God is not easily riled. He is slow to anger and incredibly patient. He doesn't grumble while waiting for his children. He doesn't hastily disfigure his enemies while defending himself. He doesn't poke his elbow into the backs of strangers. God breathes deep and puts up with a lot . . . especially from somewhat impatient me.

It Is Well

Your Peaceful God

God takes life's broken pieces and gives us
unbroken peace.

Wilbert Donald Gough

The red Jeep bounces and lurches its way along the rugged
dirt road toward the Chernobyl nuclear power plant near
the Ukraine and Byelorussian border. But the thick dust
cloud kicked up in its wake is miniscule compared with the
massive cloud that had spewed miles into the atmosphere a

few years earlier, when a violent explosion ripped apart the Chernobyl reactor on April 26, 1986.

The crippled reactor number four heaved tons of uranium fuel, cesium, plutonium, and other radioactive debris into the springtime sky. For more than a week the lethal plume carried deadly particles that, as calculated by the International Atomic Energy Agency, caused as much as four hundred times the radioactive contamination as the 1945 Hiroshima bomb.

While winds blew the airborne poisons northward across Europe, up to 70 percent of the invisible toxins rained down on unsuspecting Byelorussian citizens, trapping the Soviet republic under a blanket of latent death.

For two days the tight-lipped Communist government concealed the grave news of the tragedy from most of its own citizens and from the rest of the world. On Monday morning, April 28, Sweden set off the first alarm. They detected high levels of radiation tainting their airspace and land. Some twelve hours of stone-faced denials later, the Soviet Council of Ministers finally issued a four-sentence statement downplaying the Chernobyl accident.

For another two weeks Soviet leader Mikhail Gorbachev delayed making an official public statement. His twenty-five minute speech on Soviet television in mid-May did little to ease the pain of his people or the mistrust of the international community.

For four and a half years the Soviet officials orchestrated an international cover-up that minimized the disaster and shunned help from foreigners. During that time innocent children played in toxic streams. Uninformed fathers and mothers picked radiation-laden mushrooms in the forests and served them to their families.

Following the disaster, reports from southern Byelorussia indicated that birth defects had doubled, and chronic nose and throat illnesses had escalated tenfold. The children of Chernobyl, as they came to be known, suffered most—many from anemia, thyroid cancer, and other life-threatening diseases. Because many types of radiation and oncological diseases lie dormant for twenty years or more, these grave numbers may continue to grow. (Although today there is still controversy among scientists, doctors, and government officials worldwide over the exact long-term effects of the Chernobyl accident, no one can refute that high levels of ionizing radiation can cause illness or death.)

According to an October 1990 report by Piotr Kravchanka, the Byelorussian minister of foreign affairs to the United Nations General Assembly, at least 2.2 million Byelorussians, "including almost 800,000 children, were innocent victims of Chernobyl, hostages to the hazardous effects of radiation."

Statesman Kravchanka also admitted his government's years of silent delay: "The bitter truth is that it is only now, four and a half years later, that we are finally and with tremendous difficulty making a breach in the wall of indifference, silence, and lack of sympathy, and for this we ourselves are largely to blame."[1]

> THE LETHAL PLUME CARRIED DEADLY PARTICLES THAT CAUSED AS MUCH AS FOUR HUNDRED TIMES THE RADIOACTIVE CONTAMINATION AS THE 1945 HIROSHIMA BOMB.

Within an eighteen-mile radius of the nuclear facility, hundreds of villages eventually were declared emergency zones, and roughly two hundred thousand citizens were evacuated. Bulldozers buried entire communities under tons of soil to entomb tainted land. Some of the radioactive isotopes released on that fateful Saturday in 1986 may take a millennium to decay.

Less than three months after the 1990 UN report, I found myself crammed into the backseat of a Soviet government Jeep heading straight for the off-limits contaminated zone surrounding the still-active Chernobyl power plant.

I was a journalist traveling with an American humanitarian team delivering medicines, medical equipment, food, toys, and Bibles to the Byelorussian people. Soviet officials invited us to visit hospitals, orphanages, and farms in this ancient land of the Slavs. Everywhere we looked, people waited.

Orphaned babies and toddlers waited for someone to open their arms and homes. In the cancer wards, mothers waited on makeshift cots next to their ill children. Fathers waited for jobs on government collective farms. Doctors and nurses waited for even basic supplies of multivitamins and disposable syringes.

The word *chernobyl* in the Ukrainian and Russian languages means "mugwort" or "black, bitter grass." Eerily, the Chernobyl disaster spread acrid contaminants across the land and soured the people on the government that had lied to them for so long. Bitterness, unrest, and fear festered in the hearts and minds of the Byelorussian people while ionizing radiation broke down their immune systems.

Yet in that restless country I met people who modeled stability and calm in the tumultuous times. One of these individuals was my twenty-three-year-old interpreter, Natasha. For days I had watched her gracefully communicate between our team of seven Americans and our Soviet hosts. I admired her beautiful high cheekbones and her white fur hat, but more than anything I admired her spirit. I wanted to learn how she stayed peaceful when everything around her screamed turbulence.

As our vehicle jostles toward Chernobyl, I ask Natasha to tell me about herself. She exuberantly talks about her family and her newfound faith in God. "I used to quarrel with my grandmummy about God and an afterlife. I repeated the words of my teachers: 'There is no God.' I was like a puppet," Natasha says. "I was taught in school that the church and priests should be blamed for everything that is bad in our country."

Natasha recalls how her grandmother, a strong woman of faith, would warn Natasha not to believe her teachers' words about God, "because after teaching you there is no God, they go straight to the church to pray."

Away from home and studying at a Minsk foreign-language school, Natasha became friends with some people at a local Baptist church. They gave her a Bible.

"I have tried to read religious literature. The first time I held a Bible in my hand was last spring. I read the first pages about Adam and Eve, but it was difficult to understand," Natasha explains. "I do my best to understand because I believe in God. Sometime perhaps I will learn the Bible like the back of my hand."

After an hour of talking, Natasha's voice begins to fade. She confides that her thyroid gland is enlarged because of the continual exposure to radiation. Natasha is concerned that someday she, too, will be like the ill children we met—waiting in a hospital bed for a miracle cure. In the meantime she asks God for strength and peace to live her life fully as she waits for each new day to unfold.

"The more I see that intelligent people believe in God, the more I know that God really exists. I had some doubts about God, but now I know for sure that he's not a fairy tale," Natasha shares as she curls up and places her head on my lap. My new friend seems unfazed that we are headed straight into the area with the highest levels of radiation. In the center of the chaos threatening her health, her future, and her country, Natasha falls asleep, confident that God is on watch.

As I look back fondly on my days with Natasha, I'm reminded of someone else who rested in tranquillity while life's circumstances swirled out of control. Lawyer and real-estate investor Horatio Gates Spafford lost his four-year-old son to scarlet fever in 1870. The Chicago fire of October 1871 then wiped out his real-estate holdings along Lake Michigan and much of his wealth.

Two years later Spafford's four daughters drowned in a shipwreck off the coast of Newfoundland. His wife, Anna, survived, and together the devastated couple grieved the loss of their five children and waited for relief from their intense heartache.

Still reeling, Spafford journeyed near the spot of his daughters' accident. He penned the following words of faith and hope: "When peace, like a river, attendeth my way, When sorrows like sea billows roll; Whatever my lot, Thou has taught me to say, 'It is well, it is well, with my soul.'"

> WHILE PEACE IS PART OF GOD'S MONIKER, I ADMIT THAT MANY DAYS MY LIFE CHURNS WITH THE OPPOSITE OF PEACE.

Separated by a century and by continents, both Horatio Spafford and my friend Natasha are examples of unflappable individuals whose lives exclaim, "It is well," even as waves of waiting and uncertainty crash over them. This deep stillness of the soul comes only from God, whom the Bible calls the "God of peace" (1 Thessalonians 5:23) and the "Master of Peace" (2 Thessalonians 3:16).

While peace is part of God's moniker, I admit that many days my life churns with the opposite of peace—worry, fear, chaos, and doubt worm their way into my thoughts. As I write these words, I'm waiting for another round of diagnostic tests to rule out suspected cancer (my eighth time in twelve years). I'm squirming financially, waiting for promised checks in the mail. I'm searching for a fix to a leaking water heater that damaged my storage room and garage.

On some days I feel like my life and my emotions are in a whirling blender. The longer I wait, the more I feel like I'm chopped and puréed—a sloppy mess in God's hands. Peace of mind and heart is not my greatest trait on these days.

Peace is often thought to be a state of tranquillity or quiet, or freedom from oppressive thoughts or emotions. The Bible discusses peace at length and encourages us to "seek peace and pursue it" (Psalm 34:14) and to "live in peace" (1 Thessalonians 5:13).

But as someone who grew up in the 1960s, I'm basically desensitized to the word *peace*. I was raised in an era cluttered with the original peace signs, slapped on bell-bottoms and tie-dyed T-shirts. I yawned through President Richard Nixon's fingers raised in a V to signify peace and triumph. And one can only chuckle so many times at tongue-in-cheek bumper stickers that urge, "Pursue whirled peas." Don't even get me started on the media frenzy reporting hopes for peace in Rwanda, Bosnia, Israel, Afghanistan, and Iraq. Behind all the symbols and rhetoric, how do we secure authentic peace in this contentious world?

I'm convinced that the early Israelite settlers in the Promised Land asked the same poignant question. After leading the Jewish people to conquer Canaan, Joshua, their stalwart leader, dies. Scores of people stood with Joshua in his military campaign to win the land God earmarked for them (Genesis 12:7). But eventually that generation of faithful believers in Jehovah also passes on. Israel then plunges into a 350-year decline. Judges 2:10 informs us, "Another generation grew up, who knew neither the LORD nor what he had done for Israel."

The book of Judges chronicles the waywardness of these Israelite descendants whose lives are summed up this way: "Everyone did what was right in his own eyes" (Judges 21:25 NASB). Although the Israelites *parked* in the land of Canaan, they never fully *possessed* the land.

The first chapter in Judges is replete with accounts of the individual tribes' failures to overthrow the Canaanite strongholds. They "took possession of the hill country, but they were unable to drive the people from the plains" (v. 19), "failed to dislodge the Jebusites" (v. 21), and "did not drive out the people of Beth Shan or Taanach or Dor or Ibleam or Megiddo and their surrounding settlements" (v. 27). On and on we read of the Israelites' lackluster performance.

The Israelites passively entertained a tolerance for the pagan culture and religion of their Canaanite neighbors. In time the temple prostitution and infant sacrifice to Baal and other gods no longer seemed despicable. God's warning to Israel about the inhabitants of the land proves true: "They will be thorns in your sides and their gods will be a snare to you" (Judges 2:3).

When we tire of waiting for God to deliver us, we, too, can divert our eyes to other "helpful" sources. Weariness with waiting can nudge us subtly to make concessions to the enemy. I don't think the Canaanite Welcome Wagon volunteers whipped out free stone carvings of Baal and Ashtoreth on their first visits with their new Israelite neighbors. I think the Canaanites wooed the children of Israel bit by bit into considering other spiritual options for their lives.

When your crops lack rain, why not turn to Baal, the god of sky and rain? Surely a god who is solely responsible for clouds and storms will respond faster than a God who oversees the whole universe. Maybe the Israelites liked the notion of being able to actually see a god in the form of elaborate images and totems rather than trust the invisible God. I wonder if eventually the children of Israel viewed Jehovah as too pokey.

They wanted a god who would respond to their needs and concerns on their timetable.

Waiting for answers, and even miracles, can tempt us to jettison our true God and run to false gods. In situations that require cool-headed waiting on the Lord, we tend to heat up with anxiety and impatience. Before we know it, careless patterns creep into our lives.

We thank less and complain more. We critique and criticize God's timing. We question and blame our loved ones for our holdups. The dark nights of waiting wear us down until we forget what God has told us in the light. We let everyday circumstances and people drown out the voice of God.

If we'll listen, God's steady voice reminds us: "Be strong. Let me fight for you. Trust me. Wait for me."

But we don't listen.

Fed up with waiting, we begin to resemble the children of Israel whose devotion to Jehovah waxed and waned. These loose-living people were ruled for nearly four centuries by a series of seventeen judges who were both military and civil leaders. Despite the judges' attempts to rally the people to resist their Canaanite enemies, Israel acquiesced and "prostituted themselves to other gods and worshiped them. Unlike their fathers, they quickly turned from the way in which their fathers had walked, the way of obedience to the LORD's commands" (Judges 2:17).

Life during the time of the judges was not exactly stable and serene. Reading about this period of Israel's history is like enduring a seventy-mile-per-hour harrowing spin on the Viper, one of the world's largest looping roller coasters. For a number of years Israel rides high on God's provision of rest. But then they abandon God and descend into years of domination by other nations. The tumultuous cycle went like this: eight years of slavery, forty years of rest; eighteen years of slavery, eighty years of rest; twenty years of slavery, forty years of rest.

But then, in Judges 6, we encounter a man named Gideon who is secretly threshing wheat to save it from being plundered by the ruling Midianites. Israel is toiling through the seventh year of yet another low point in the cycle when God chooses to appoint Gideon to be the new judge. Gideon's Hebrew name means "great warrior, smiter, or feller," so apparently Gideon can hold his own against the opposition.

Yet as soon the angel of the Lord meets Gideon, this son of Joash questions God's ability to show up on time: "If the LORD is with us, why has all this happened to us? Where are all his wonders that our fathers told us about when they said, 'Did not the LORD bring us up out of Egypt?' But now the LORD has abandoned us and put us into the hand of Midian" (Judges 6:13).

Sounds a lot like Gideon's ancestors after they escaped Egypt. (Remember their laments in chapter 1 of this book?) When waiting, even tough guys can feel deserted by God. Notice the Lord's calm response to Gideon. "The LORD looked at him and said, 'Go in this your strength and deliver Israel from the hand of Midian. Have I not sent you?'" (Judges 6:14 NASB).

Can't you just imagine the Almighty giving his handpicked servant "the look"? You know the look I'm talking about: a slight eye roll and a raised eyebrow followed by the stare. The stare parents unleash on their rebellious kids. The stare that penetrates smoke and mirrors.

Trying another tactic to negotiate his way out of leading his countrymen, Gideon pleads with God, in effect, "Look, my family is from the other side of the tracks, and I'm the baby in the family. I know you appreciate youthful enthusiasm, but surely you don't think *I* qualify for your service."

Excuses, excuses. We all make them, whether God wants us to wait or step out in faith. When it comes to waiting, we tell God that we're not equipped to handle long delays. We remind him that we don't have the constitution necessary to endure.

But God is unfazed by empty excuses and unsound rebuttals. He'd heard the inadequacy defense from Moses centuries before (Exodus 3–4). God didn't budge. He lovingly assures Gideon, "I will be with you" (Judges 6:16). God promises his unfailing presence to Gideon—and he does the same for us today.

Gideon still hedges and tries to bargain with God. He begs for a sign to know for sure that God is the one handing down the orders. Bargaining with God seems part of our human nature. When waiting and wondering backs us into a corner, we call out to God for "a sign for good" (Psalm 86:17 NASB). We long for tangible proof that God still cares and wants to intervene on our behalf.

> WHEN WAITING AND WONDERING BACKS US INTO A CORNER, WE LONG FOR TANGIBLE PROOF THAT GOD STILL CARES AND WANTS TO INTERVENE ON OUR BEHALF.

Now, remember, Gideon lived in a wicked, whacky time. Baal worshipers routinely slaughtered their children; the Midianites ravaged the land and "ruined the crops all the way to Gaza and did not spare a living thing for Israel, neither sheep nor cattle nor donkeys" (Judges 6:4). The people were surrounded by unrest and unruliness, not peace and prosperity.

After more than two hundred years of vacillating between God and Baal and his idol cronies, Israel needs another wake-up call. The Lord shows Gideon a visible sign of divine power on earth. God torches Gideon's meat-and-bread offering, then proclaims, "Peace! Do not be afraid" (Judges 6:23).

Gideon builds an altar on the spot and names it, in Hebrew, *Yahweh-shalom*, or "The LORD is Peace" (Judges 6:24). This is the first time in all of Scripture that we see God identified as *Yahweh-shalom* or *Jehovah-shalom*—at the precise moment in Israel's turbulent history when Gideon and his entire nation need to recognize and celebrate God's divine character of peace. Notice that verse 24 says God *is* peace. Not just a God who prays for peace or extends peace. God is peace.

"When the hour is dark and the situation desperate," wrote Bible teacher and author Kay Arthur, "we finally long for God's peace. Then we crave it. Our sanity depends on it. Fear grips us. We grope through the darkness, longing for peace's reassurance that everything will be all right."[2]

Can you relate to longing for God's peace? To knowing your very sanity depends on his ability to blanket you with his stability and serenity? I believe Gideon could.

After God emboldens Gideon's spirit with peace, this clandestine wheat grinder turns into a valiant warrior, leading Israel on a thrilling victory over Midian with the help of just three hundred men armed with torches, pitchers, and trumpets. It's amazing what a true perception of God can do to change the course of world history.

Just before Jesus is about to alter the ages through his death on the cross, he bolsters his disciples' courage with these words: "Peace I leave with you; my peace I give you. I do not give to you as the world gives. Do not let your hearts be troubled and do not be afraid" (John 14:27). God's peace far exceeds the peace treaties and few tranquil moments the world manages to secure.

World-renowned evangelist Billy Graham illustrated true peace in the story of a raging storm that sent massive waves crashing against shoreline rocks. Lightning ripped through darkened skies, thunder cracked for miles, and the winds howled with ferocious intensity. Yet in a crevice in the rocks, a tiny bird slept with its head nestled serenely under its wing. "That is peace: to be able to sleep in the storm! In Christ we are relaxed and at peace in the midst of the confusions, bewilderments, and perplexities of this life," Graham said. "The storm rages, but our hearts are at rest. We have found peace—at last!"[3]

This story reminds me of when Jesus and his disciples are lashed by fierce gales on the Sea of Galilee. Roaring waves smash over their boat, flooding the vessel with chilly water. But what is Jesus doing while his men scream for their lives? The "Prince of Peace" (Isaiah 9:6) "was in the stern, sleeping on a cushion" (Mark 4:38). In the height of the tempest, the serene Master and Commander catches some z's.

Of course that didn't last long. The disciples rouse Jesus from his deep slumber and accuse, "Teacher, don't you care if we drown?" (Mark 4:38). Duh! But you know what? We hurl the same accusation at God every time we doubt his concern or timely intervention in our affairs. "Hello! Wake up, God. Get with the program here. I'm about to be tossed overboard. How much longer do you expect me to wait? Hello-o-o. Are you sleeping?"

I imagine the Messiah simply yawning through his disciples' panic. He commands the wind and waves: "Quiet! Be still!" Instantly the fury stops. Nature and humanity are again at peace.

I've never experienced a storm at sea, but growing up in the Midwest, I've shuddered through countless thunderstorms. As a little girl tucked in my bed at night, I tried to bravely endure the booming and crashing of many a cloudburst. But no matter how hard I pressed my pillow over my eyes and ears, I couldn't block out the blazing lightning and the violent thunder that rattled my bedroom windows.

Overwhelmed by fear, I did the only thing I knew would calm my racing heart. I scurried down the hallway and slipped into my parents' bed. Sometimes I plopped right in the middle of Mom and Dad, but usually I'd find Dad on his side, with his arm outstretched over the bed's edge. Gingerly I would lift up his forearm and slide under it, snuggling against his chest. Secure under my father's "wing," I was safe. I fell asleep peacefully, even with the monstrous storm still raging.

The Message poignantly describes a similar experience in David's life: "I've run to you for dear life. I'm hiding out under your wings until the hurricane blows over. I call out to High God, the God who holds me together" (Psalm 57:1–2).

Hiding out under God's wings—the God who holds us together. What better place could we be when the torrential rains and shrill winds of waiting rail against us?

Do horrendous squalls of delay threaten to uproot your faith in life . . . in others . . . in God? Is your wait leaving you drenched with fear, exhaustion, and despair?

"We must wait for God, long, meekly, in the wind and wet, in the thunder and lightning, in the cold and the dark," explained hymnist Frederick W. Faber. "Wait, and he will come."⁴

No matter how unruly, cold, or dark life gets, your Jehovah-shalom will come. He left the river for Mary and Martha, showed up at a threshing machine for Gideon, and halted the storm for his disciples.

He soothed Natasha's spirit in a land plagued with deadly radiation. He reassured Horatio, who had lost five children, that despite the rolling sea billows, peace would attend his way.

In your season of waiting, may you rest in God's peace so that you, too, can confidently say, "It is well with my soul."

"Now may the Lord of peace himself give you peace at all times and in every way" (2 Thessalonians 3:16).

Just Being There
Your Comforting God

God does not comfort us to make us comfortable,
but to make us comforters.

John Henry Jowett

At 2:14 p.m. Continental Flight 1713 noses into takeoff
position at Denver's Stapleton International Airport. Howling,
subzero winds and a swirling sea of snow pelt the plane. Flight
attendant Kelly Engelhart straps herself into a jump seat at the
rear of the plane. The idling aircraft, delayed by ice buildup on
the wings, is finally cleared for its journey to Boise, Idaho.

For the next sixty seconds the thunderous DC-9 rumbles down the runway, accelerating to a speed of 170 miles per hour. As the plane's nose lifts, Kelly sighs to herself, *We're OK.*

But her optimism is short-lived. Barely a hundred feet in the air, Flight 1713 lurches and begins shuddering violently. The right wing dips downward; the fuselage jerks and rolls to the left.

> THE SEASONED FLIGHT ATTENDANT SHUTS HER EYES AND PICTURES THE FACE OF JESUS. "HERE I COME, LORD. HERE I COME."

"We're going down! We're going down!" yells Chris Metts, the flight attendant seated to Kelly's right. "Pray, Kelly. Pray!" The two flying partners reach out to brace each other.

Kelly's thoughts instantly turn to her husband and their preschool daughter and son. *I'll never see them again. I can't believe this is my time to die!*

The aircraft's left wing rips into the frozen ground, shredding both metal and earth. Passengers scream frantically at the deafening sound of explosions. Out of the chaos a massive orange fireball blasts down the aisle toward Kelly. The seasoned flight attendant instinctively shuts her eyes and pictures the face of Jesus. "Here I come, Lord. Here I come," she whispers faintly.

With horrifying sounds of crunching and destruction, the plane skids, pushing piles of snow and dirt into the shattered fuselage and hurling passengers across the cabin to collide with debris and other bodies. Five-foot-two-inch Kelly is slammed against her shoulder harness. She tucks her head as ice and gravel rip into her face.

Within seconds the roaring airplane flips like a plastic toy. The DC-9 cartwheels on its wing tip and crashes, upside down, to the ground. Then, an engulfing, eerie silence.

Hanging upside down in her seat, Kelly opens her eyes and squints into the smoky darkness. The speeding fireball she'd feared would sear her alive in the twisted, fuel-soaked cabin . . . somehow just vanished.

The plane's carcass lies in scattered pieces—the crash sheared off the cockpit cabin, left wing, and tail. The main cabin lies splayed open from its wings backward.

"At that point I could not believe that we were alive," Kelly later tells me, speaking of those harrowing moments waiting to cross from life to death or somehow survive. "I felt such a presence of God around the plane."

Chris and Kelly roll out of their seats and immediately turn to post-crash duties. Chris, with the help of some uninjured passengers, props open the rear door, and those who can, scramble out into the swirling blizzard.

Looking back on that terrifying afternoon of November 15, 1987, Kelly remembers the surge of emotions as she walks away from the burning wreckage. "I grabbed the first person I saw and cried, "We made it. This is a miracle. We should never have made it. It's a miracle!"

Seconds after escaping the wreckage, Kelly scurries around the plane bolstering other survivors' spirits as they all wait agonizing minutes for rescue workers to arrive. The walking wounded desperately need medical attention, and other passengers are still pinned between twisted seats and tangled metal. Battling the frigid wind and snow only intensifies the difficulty of their wait.

Numbed by the horrifying ordeal and the freezing temperatures, Kelly kneels in the snowstorm beside a sobbing woman. Kelly removes her flight attendant's jacket and gently wraps it around the distraught passenger.

In the intense moments after a dreadful accident that killed twenty-eight people—but miraculously spared fifty-four others—one sacrificial act stands out. A bruised and scraped-up flight attendant knelt down in the snow and placed her own jacket on another hurting woman. In spite of her own discomfort, Kelly Engelhart chose to extend soothing comfort to a stranger.

I don't know how I would have handled surviving a catastrophic airplane crash and then waiting and waiting in a winter storm for someone to come to my aid. I'm a woman who chomps at the bit just waiting at stoplights. And I hate to be cold!

Thankfully, Kelly didn't let her own suffering stop her. Her story is a tremendous example of stepping outside our own needs to ease the distress and anxiety of others. Kelly did not learn this selfless willingness to console people from Continental Airlines. She modeled what she'd learned from her Father.

In 2 Corinthians 1:3–4 God is called "the Father of compassion and the God of all comfort, who comforts us in all our troubles, so that we can comfort those in any trouble with the comfort we ourselves have received from God."

The "God of all comfort" is someone we all need, but especially when we're limping and crawling our way through an agonizing wait. Think about the times you've had to tarry before God and wait for him to respond. What helped you endure the slowly ticking clock? I know what helps me: God's comfort expressed through people—by a hug, a prayer, a shared Bible verse, a silly card, or a hearty laugh.

———

A number of years ago I caught a powerful glimpse of God's comfort on earth. I learned of an amazing community who lived out Jesus's words in Matthew 5:4, "Blessed are those who mourn, for they will be comforted."

I can still recall that damp night, women and young children crouching around the mattress of Consolata Nakafeero, dead from AIDS. A mother wails and rocks, cries and moans, leading a cadence of mourning. Grief shrouds the hut and the entire village of Kigenya, Uganda.

Outside restless men poke at a fire while others toss and turn on clammy beds of banana leaves. The wails of the women slice through the darkness, challenging the African dawn.

As the morning sun peeks through the *mtokwe* trees, the women wrap Consolata in bark cloth. A handful of men carve out a grave behind her home and lower her into it. One by one, villagers drop handfuls of dirt into the grave. For the people of Kigenya—where more than half of the adult population had tested positive for HIV—death lurks nearby, a constant part of village life. In Kigenya everyone loses someone to the disease.

My photographer friend Susie, who visited Kigenya to work on a magazine feature, describes the villagers' response to death as "a ministry of presence unlike I've seen anywhere inside or outside the Church. As a community they respond in being there for each other."

Cultures around the world respond differently to the loss of loved ones, but a comforting "ministry of presence" is something we can all appreciate. When my mother died, my cousin Bev and her husband, Dan, were the first people to show up at my parents' home. A few years earlier they had lost their nineteen-year-old daughter in a car accident. Dan and Bev didn't try to soothe us with "we've been there too" litanies. They simply sat with us for an hour or so and let the conversation ebb and flow.

I can't remember specifically what we talked about that morning, but I do remember those relatives just being there. Like the people of Kigenya, Dan and Bev extended comfort by just showing up.

We see these same consoling actions demonstrated in the Old

Testament, in relation to the godly man Job. The Bible portrays Job as "blameless and upright; he feared God and shunned evil. . . . He was the greatest man among all the people of the East" (Job 1:1, 3). That's quite a reputation! We read about this noble man in the book of the Bible that bears his name.

> WE MUST ALWAYS REMEMBER, ESPECIALLY WHEN WE'RE WALLOWING IN A SWAMP OF WAITING, THAT OUR LOVING GOD SCREENS EVERYTHING WE FACE.

In Job's day, people's wealth is based on the quantity of their livestock, not their silver and gold. Job employs a host of servants and owns seven thousand sheep, three thousand camels, five hundred pairs of oxen, and five hundred donkeys. The grand total of his herds: eleven thousand five hundred animals. (I sure hope the winds blew downwind from his barns and away from his house.)

Job enjoys his seven sons and three daughters, and as a God-honoring father, he regularly rises early in the morning to "sacrifice a burnt offering for each of them, thinking, 'Perhaps my children have sinned and cursed God in their hearts'" (Job 1:5).

Satan doesn't like the wholesomeness of Job or his squeaky-clean lifestyle. So the wily one asks the Almighty for permission to rough up Job and test his loyalty to God.

It's crucial to note that the evil one bows in submission to God's ruling authority. Often when we feel roughed up by life and have to wait for some relief, some answer, some healing, we wrestle with our view of God. In life's delays, while we suffer, does God have the upper hand, or does the devil? God allows Satan some freedom to challenge

Job, but we must always remember, especially when we're wallowing in a swamp of waiting, that our loving God screens everything we face.

Next, in verses 13–19, we discover Satan's assault on Job with unfathomable tragedies. In one day he loses every one of his ten children, all his livestock, and all but a handful of his servants. Most of us can't begin to imagine the unbearable shock and sorrow Job suffers. I'm always awed when I read how Job handled these horrific losses: "Through all this Job did not sin nor did he blame God" (Job 1:22 NASB).

Remember the "but God" phrase from chapter 1? If I were Job, I probably would grill God with, "But God, how could you ruin me like this? But God, why me? I'm such a close follower of yours. But God, how will I ever survive this wretched pain?"

When Job refuses to let his faith in his Creator falter, Satan is permitted to afflict Job with tormenting boils from head to toe. We read of Job's ensuing misery and grief in Job 2:11–13:

> When Job's three friends, Eliphaz the Temanite, Bildad the Shuhite and Zophar the Naamathite, heard about all the troubles that had come upon him, they set out from their homes and met together by agreement to go and sympathize with him and comfort him. When they saw him from a distance, they could hardly recognize him; they began to weep aloud, and they tore their robes and sprinkled dust on their heads. Then they sat on the ground with him for seven days and seven nights. No one said a word to him, because they saw how great his suffering was.

Job's three buddies from different countries determine to "sympathize with him and comfort him." Note the simple words in verse 13: "they sat on the ground with him for seven days and seven nights. No one said a word."

145

Now, that's a ministry of presence and a ministry of waiting. These guys don't check Job and themselves into a luxurious hotel room with a wide-screen TV. They don't pull up overstuffed couches or recliners. They don't hit the hot tub, shoot some hoops, or go off-roading in their souped-up chariots.

The four men just hunker down on the ground . . . in silence . . . for nearly 170 hours. (Sorry, gals, but I know of no woman who'd even attempt that!) And this no-talk gathering around Job is no feat to set a Guinness World Record or to win at *Survivor: The Land of Uz*. Eliphaz, Bildad, and Zophar are three amigos who just want to comfort their hurting friend.

We later find that these comrades try to console Job with their pious admonitions, but undoubtedly, their greatest blessing to Job comes before they open their mouths. True comfort often comes without words: a jacket around the shoulder, a visit without pep talks.

In your own time of waiting through grief, disappointment, and myriad unknowns, you might not experience loved ones sitting with you in silence for an entire week. But perhaps a select few will respond like my cousins or like Consolata Nakafeero's people—by just showing up to help ease the burden.

I can recall a number of times when my close friends showed up just when I needed them most. One night in particular I was writhing on the living room floor with excruciating sciatic pain down both legs. I describe this torture as a root canal multiplied by one hundred. As I sobbed from the agony, a dear friend got down on the floor with me and enfolded me in an embrace. Weeping on her shoulder brought comfort in my exhausting onslaught of pain.

A year or so later I returned the comfort when I sat next to this friend on her couch in silence as she cried her way through an emotionally distressing situation. No words . . . just a touch of the hand . . . an understanding heart.

In distressing times, my friend and I often turn to the psalmist's timeless message that speaks to finding comfort in God's Word: "My comfort in my suffering is this: Your promise preserves my life. . . . I remember your ancient laws, O LORD, and I find comfort in them" (Psalm 119:50, 52).

While many of us choose to seek comfort in our Creator, it helps to also let down our guard and admit our need to people he's placed in our lives. An early episode of the television series *Judging Amy* illustrates this truth. Vincent's girlfriend, Carol, stops by his place and opens up about her family and friends who rely on her strength and her financial and practical help.

Wearied from overextending herself at times, Carol begins to cry. Nearly choking on her tears, Carol sputters, "Everybody loves strong people because they never need anything. But it doesn't mean they don't have needs."

Carol sobs harder, and Vincent gently asks, "What do you need right now?"

Relieved by his comforting words, Carol leans on Vincent's shoulder and whispers, "To be a mess." Then, after a moment, she adds, "And maybe a little chocolate would help."[1]

When we face challenging circumstances and grow weary of plodding on under such a heavy burden, we certainly can feel like we want to just break down and be a mess. Sometimes, when time drags on without our consent and we don't know when—or if—things will get better, we *are* a mess. But it's OK, especially if we know that some form of comfort is on its way.

It's been said that "not a sigh is breathed, not a pain felt, not a grief pierces the soul, but the throb vibrates to the Father's heart."[2] I am certain that the horrendous 9/11 attacks on America caused God's heart to throb with sorrow. Not one sigh or moan of agony on that fateful day or the anguishing days to follow escaped God's notice.

Two weeks after terrorists rammed airplanes into the World Trade Center, the Pentagon, and a Pennsylvania field, I had the privilege of interviewing two women who lost their husbands in the September 11, 2001, catastrophe. One, Lisa Beamer, became a national symbol of courage and hope; the other stayed behind the scenes but shared an equally tenacious faith.

> NOT ONE SIGH OR MOAN OF AGONY ON THAT FATEFUL DAY OR THE ANGUISHING DAYS TO FOLLOW ESCAPED GOD'S NOTICE.

On that unforgettable Tuesday morning, Shelly Genovese is still asleep when her visiting mother bolts into the bedroom Shelly shares with her husband, Steve. Shelly's mom alerts her that American Flight 11 has dozed into Tower One of the World Trade Center. A partner with the financial services company Cantor Fitzgerald, Steve works on the 104th floor— six floors from the top of this majestic landmark of international trade.

The aircraft decimates the structure about ten floors below Steve's office. Just before Shelly's mom wakes her, Steve calls from work and leaves a phone message, blurting, "Shelly, wake up! Answer the phone! I think a plane just hit my building! Turn on the TV. Wake up!" When Shelly checks her phone messages and hears her husband's voice, she quickly reasons, *Steve called. He's fine.*

After the 1993 World Trade Center bombing, Steve had walked

down dozens of flights of stairs. He'd survived that attack on the stately skyscraper, so Shelly counts on his escaping to safety again.

The house soon fills with concerned neighbors and friends. Shelly keeps telling herself, *He's gonna call. He's gonna call.* Everyone in the Genovese home that day waits for the phone to ring. They wait for the father of sixteen-month-old Jacqueline Lea to call on his cell phone and whisper "I love you" to his daughter and to his wife of nearly five years. They wait for the gregarious NASDAQ trader to come walking through the door.

With anxious hope they wait, huddled around the television like millions of other Americans. They let out a collective moan when, at 9:03 a.m., a second airplane smashes into Tower Two, and again when it collapses almost an hour later.

Shelly continues reassuring herself, *He still has time to get down. He still has time to get down.* At 10:28 a.m., when Steve's building crumbles into a massive heap of crushed concrete and steel, Shelly falls to her knees, screaming.

"Then I just felt this peace about me," Shelly says later of that terrifying moment. "I know the peace came from God. I just felt like Steve was OK. We always read Psalm 91 together, so I pulled out my Bible and read that psalm. The end of Psalm 91 talks about God rescuing and giving everlasting life. Those verses truly just comforted me."

Facing one of the most gut-wrenching experiences in her nation's history, Shelly Genovese finds comfort in God and in his Word: "I will say of the LORD, 'He is my refuge and my fortress, my God, in whom I trust.' . . . He will command his angels concerning you to guard you in all your ways; they will lift you up in their hands" (Psalm 91:2, 11–12).

Though Steve was one of 658 Cantor Fitzgerald employees who

never made it out of their office building on that tragic Tuesday, his wife rested in the peace of knowing that their God—an impenetrable refuge and fortress—would send his angels to comfort and console.

On that same September morning, just a few miles south of the Twin Towers, author and *Newsweek* columnist Anna Quindlen sat alone in her Victorian row house, watching the horrible events unfold on television. Anna later wrote in her book *Loud and Clear*:

> I knew something uniquely terrible was taking place. I also had reason to believe that everyone I cared for most was safe: My husband across the Hudson at his office. The children at their schools. My friend in the hospital across town. It was difficult for us to talk to one another, of course, with the New York City telephone lines out, the tunnels and bridges shut down, and cyberspace hopelessly jammed. One of the mementos I have kept from that morning are three identical e-mails from our son at college, who could not get through on the day of his birthday or for three days afterward. Each one is dated September 11, 2001, and says in capital letters I REALLY NEED TO HEAR YOUR VOICE.[3]

I REALLY NEED TO HEAR YOUR VOICE . . . I REALLY NEED TO HEAR YOUR VOICE . . . I REALLY NEED TO HEAR YOUR VOICE. It's the cry of every comfortless soul who feels cut off from the world, hampered by circumstances of delay.

If it were possible, I suspect Mary and Martha would type the same desperate e-mail message to Jesus or send a text message to his cell phone. "Lazarus is dying. We really need to hear your voice . . . see your face. Come now."

During their desperate hours of loss and grief, the sisters long for the comfort of their friend and Lord. In John 11:19 we read, "Many

Jews had come to Martha and Mary to comfort them in the loss of their brother." Part of a tight-knit Jewish community, Lazarus's sisters are surrounded by fellow mourners.

No doubt relatives, neighbors, and townspeople show up with mounds of fresh bread cakes and just-picked figs. (Because every funeral seems to call for casseroles, Mary and Martha must have to write at least one thank-you note for a Lamb and Lentil Surprise.)

I can just hear all the Jewish moms, in their thick Judean accents, urging the forlorn sisters to keep up their strength with some food. "Come on, girls, just eat . . . e-e-eat. You're gonna waste away. E-e-e-eat."

I'm guessing those sisters are a mess. But no amount of delectable food or words of concern can lift Martha and Mary out of their grief. They want the comfort that only their Messiah can give. They want to hear his voice—they want his ministry of presence.

The minutes stretch to hours and the hours to days. Mary and Martha attend to final details and to the burial of their precious brother. They no doubt appreciate the outpouring of love of family and friends, but one might imagine that nothing can soothe the deep bruising of Mary's and Martha's souls.

Four days after Lazarus is laid to rest, Jesus approaches Bethany. Word reaches Martha, and she hurries to meet her long-expected friend. Mary, however, stays home, probably shrouded in inconsolable grief.

Just being with Jesus is enough to lighten the heaviness of Martha's sorrow, but Jesus does more. He reassures Martha of his power over death and promises to raise Lazarus from the grave. Martha scurries to share the news with her sister.

Note Martha's words to Mary in John 11:28: "'The Teacher is here,' she said, 'and is asking for you.'" What a joyful report! What uplifting words of comfort. *Jesus is here! I get to hear his voice. I get to see him once again. He's asking for me.*

This same Jesus from Nazareth wants to comfort you in your difficult seasons of waiting. He longs to show up and calm you with his ministry of presence.

I love how Jesus comforts his comrades with this ministry of presence in some of his final moments on earth. The final chapter of John offers a touching glimpse of Jesus just being there for his hurting friends.

The disciples are still reeling from the tremendous disappointment and public humiliation of watching their leader die, condemned as an outlaw. For three years these gung-ho men journeyed with Jesus across the sands and waters of Palestine only to see Jesus beaten and crucified.

But suddenly he is back, alive, and making guest appearances to those who fondly call on his name.

In John 21 we find a group of disciples who, dazed by the loss of Jesus, need the comfort of the familiar to help them cope. So they hit the water. Simon Peter, formerly a fisherman by trade, declares, "I'm going out to fish" (John 21:3). His longtime fishing buddies, James and John, the sons of fisherman Zebedee, hop into the boat with Simon. So does Thomas, Nathanael, and two other unnamed disciples. There's something to be said for getting outdoors when grief makes life crawl along slower than a slug.

The disciples fish all night on the Sea of Tiberias, better known as the Sea of Galilee. In the region around this popular freshwater lake, Jesus had three years earlier called several disciples to join him in the adventure of a lifetime. As a geographical focal point of much of Jesus's ministry, the lake feels like home to the disciples. They know every fishing hot spot on that nearly thirteen-mile stretch of water, but by sunrise they have caught not even one fish.

Then, from along the shore, a stranger calls to them and directs them to cast their net on the right side of the boat. Maybe a little reluctant to follow unsolicited advice, the men heave their net into the water anyway—and land so many fish they almost can't haul in the net.

John then recognizes their fishing guide as Jesus. Notice in verse 7 what Simon Peter does. Delighted to see Jesus and eager to get to him, Simon jumps into the water and starts splashing his way to his Master.

Oh, if only we had this kind of desire to meet with Jesus. If only, in the murky waters of waiting, we would abandon our ship of self-effort and race to our God.

THERE'S SOMETHING TO BE SAID FOR GETTING OUTDOORS WHEN GRIEF MAKES LIFE CRAWL ALONG SLOWER THAN A SLUG.

One of my favorite scenes in all of Scripture unfolds next. When the disciples really need to hear Jesus's voice and see his face, Jesus takes time to encourage them and to just be there with his friends. He knows they are exhausted and famished, so he builds a fire and fixes them some charbroiled comfort food. "Jesus said to them, 'Come and have breakfast.' None of the disciples dared ask him, 'Who are you?' They knew it was the Lord" (John 21:12).

How about you? Do you know it's the Lord when you feel a cool breeze of comfort? Are you learning to recognize God's sometimes subtle and sometimes sensational ways of being with you in your times of waiting? You just never know when the God of all comfort might show up with a warm embrace, a message from his Word, or a meal from heaven.

Not Yet

Your In-Control God

All this teaching about God's sovereignty can be hard
to buy. But listen . . . You either buy it or you don't.
Either God is in control, or he's not.

Kay Arthur

Sprawled on his belly, Captain Scott O'Grady presses himself
down into the damp Bosnian soil. With green flight gloves
draped over his face and eyes for camouflage, the U.S. Air Force
pilot freezes, barely breathing. His heart thumps wildly.

Two pursuers creep by just five feet away. Over the next
hour, a dozen or more armed Bosnian Serbs stomp through

the low bushes and skinny trees hiding the camouflaged American. The twenty-nine-year-old captain literally holds his breath and waits. Silently he prays.

As one of thirty-five American pilots assigned to the 555th Fighter Squadron stationed at Aviona Air Base in northeast Italy, Scott left the air base at 1:15 that Friday afternoon, June 2, 1995. Accompanied by a lead pilot, wingman Scott flies his forty-seventh routine mission over the land of battling Serbs, Muslims, and Croats.

> THE STUNNED PILOT EXPECTS THE COCKPIT TO EXPLODE AT ANY SECOND. HE PRAYS, *DEAR GOD, DON'T LET ME DIE.*

After circling in cloudy skies over Bosnia and Herzegovina, a shrill alarm sounds in Scott's cockpit at 3:03 p.m.—the enemy's ground radar has targeted him. Within seconds the Bosnian Serbs launch two surface-to-air missiles.

The first missile misses Scott's F-16; the second one pierces the underbelly, ramming into one of the fuel tanks and slicing the plane in two. Intense fire and searing heat engulfs the cockpit as the crippled plane pitches and rolls out of control.

The jet's nose and cockpit—with Scott hunched down inside—rip away from the rest of the plane. He feels flames lick his cheeks and the back of his neck. The stunned pilot expects the cockpit to explode at any second. He prays, *Dear God, don't let me die.*

Even as those words form in his dazed mind, Scott looks down and grabs the ejection handle. Soaring five miles above the earth at five hundred miles per hour, the airman ejects into the freezing atmosphere.

Still strapped to his ACES II ejection seat, the free-falling pilot manually deploys his parachute. For the next twenty-five minutes Scott senses he is trapped in a surreal time warp. His slow descent leaves him vulnerable to the enemy below. Over and over the pilot prays for God's protection.

Scott glances to the south, where what remains of his plane sends out thick, black smoke. Are soldiers and locals already at the site, poking around the debris and looking for the pilot's charred body?

The injured serviceman lands in a grassy clearing surrounded by woods. Spotting an enemy military truck and car, apparently following his descending parachute, Scott knows that staying in the open means risking either quick death or prolonged torture.

Scott unclips his parachute, scoops up his survival rucksack, and races toward a grove of trees for cover. The burns on his face sting, but he discerns few other injuries. The emotional strain of the previous hour quickly exhausts him, and he collapses in a fetal position.

Nearby the sounds of vehicles and hurried voices draw closer. The American captain grabs his two-way radio and calls for help. No reply.

He tries again, then shuts off the radio as more vehicles roar by his landing site. As footsteps approach, Scott fears enemy capture.

"When I heard them fire off their weapons that first evening, around the area I was hiding—that certainly scared me," Scott recounts. "I was not sure I was going to get out of there if they did capture me, because I thought they'd just put a bullet in my head."

For six hours Scott lies motionless against the moist dirt, thinking of his family, his God, and his plan for surviving. "I felt peace in my heart knowing that even if the next funeral I attended was my own, I would have eternal peace with God, and that was uplifting," Scott later reflects. "Gaining that perspective turned the situation around for me. I was in a cautious state, but I was elated with positive strength, believing that I would get through."

At daybreak Scott drinks from his Flexipak—his first liquid in seventeen hours. Sore and stiff, he sneaks a short distance to a new hideout. The abundance of low tree branches there will better conceal him from the Serbs searching for him by air and on foot.

Painstakingly studying his issued topographical map, Scott identifies a hill that could serve as a landing spot for rescuers. To reach the hill, some two miles away, Scott devises a plan to travel at night. Pressing himself to the ground, motionless, Scott passes the lonely daylight hours under a shelter of green tarp and camouflage netting.

Following his military survival training, the pilot nibbles on tree leaves. His water packs are exhausted after two days, so Scott traps meager raindrops in a plastic bag. He pops squirming ants into his parched mouth. He munches on grass. He wrings out his sweat-soaked socks and brushes his lips with the moisture.

Scott's several attempts to monitor his radio for any signs of an approaching rescue prove ineffective. Eventually, the captain turns on his radio's high-pitched universal distress beacon. A few minutes later he hears a faint voice say in English, ". . . heard some beacons . . . see if you . . ." Scott rejoices, knowing that he is now in range of radio messages and that NATO troops are looking for him.

The U.S. military saw no parachutes emerge from the flaming debris, so they declare Scott missing in action. But then search-and-rescue pilots start picking up a beacon signal from the general area where Scott's plane crashed. Scott's family, waiting anxiously several thousand miles away in America, hears this news on Monday—news that kindles their hope and fortifies their spirits during their grueling wait.

Before daylight on Wednesday, Scott crawls over low rock walls and through small fields below the hill that is his goal. He sets up his GPS receiver, fixes his coordinates, and flicks on his beacon for a few seconds. For an hour he waits, listening for the sound of a human voice.

Finally, on Alpha channel, he detects three sharp clicks—a sign that someone is trying to call him. At 2:08 a.m. on Thursday, an American Air Force pilot flying about seventy-five miles from Scott's crash site hears through his headset Scott's voice: "I'm alive, I'm alive!" Within minutes a forty-two-member tactical recovery team stationed on an assault ship in the Adriatic Sea kicks into high gear to rescue the downed pilot.

Scott knows it was possible the Serbs have intercepted his radio transmissions, so he is shocked and dismayed when, at 2:45 a.m., he learns that NATO wants to wait for the cover of darkness the following evening to rescue him. "No. Get me the heck out of here now!" Scott shouts into his radio. To the chilled and beleaguered pilot who has endured six days behind enemy lines, waiting no longer seems like an option.

In a grand air rescue that no Hollywood moviemaker could have imagined better, two Super Stallion helicopters, two Cobra assault helicopters, and a complete fleet of heavy-duty military aircraft swoop through fog banks over the Bosnian countryside.

About 6:40 a.m. the two Super Stallions land roughly two hundred yards from Scott. As U.S. Marines fan out over the hilltop with their M-16s, ready to take out any enemy combatants, the adrenaline-charged Scott zigzags through the woods and scrambles into one of the Super Stallions.

With their mission on the ground complete, the two Super Stallions lift off at 6:48 a.m. and head west toward the Adriatic Sea. But just when Scott and his rescuers think they are safe, Serb antiaircraft artillery rip through the skies, damaging the main rotor and tail blade of the helicopter carrying Scott. Enemy fire continues for five stressful minutes, then abruptly stops. The low-flying Stallion clears Bosnian airspace at 7:15 a.m.

Finally, Scott's harrowing wait is over. At 7:29 a.m. on June 8, after nearly a week of fear, desperation, and courage, the captain steps out of the Super Stallion into a throng of well-wishers aboard the USS *Kearsarge*.

A team of U.S. Navy doctors scrub and poke the rescued pilot and determine that his most serious medical condition is trench foot, caused by prolonged exposure to the cold and damp. Fortunately, the second-degree burns on his neck and cheek and his multiple scrapes and bruises are not infected. The exhausted-but-elated pilot has dropped twenty-five pounds but would soon be back to full strength. At one of Scott's many welcome-home celebrations, then Secretary of Defense William Perry exclaims, "They shot his plane down, but not his spirit."

UNDERSTANDING GOD'S NATURE HELPS US TO APPRECIATE HIS ABSOLUTE CONTROL.

Since his narrow escape in 1995, the easygoing pilot has developed a richer understanding of the God who directed his steps across hostile enemy terrain. Now a seminary student and traveling speaker, Scott's tenacious spirit is evident every time he stands before an audience to share his remarkable survival story. He credits his in-control God for truly saving his life.

"Everything that happens in our lives, even the bad things, God has a purpose for them. God loves us and is totally in control," the military hero explained in a telephone interview. "I am better for having gone through tough times than if I had never experienced them, because otherwise I would never have experienced and known God's true character."

Waiting six days for rescue or death taught downed pilot Scott O'Grady to cling to his faith in God's power. Understanding God's nature helps us to appreciate his absolute control over enemy missiles, sunshine and rainfall, and the most sophisticated rescue aircraft. Even the tiny ants Scott ate were under the direction of the Almighty.

Late Christian leader Bill Bright spoke often of God's being the director of our individual lives. For a number of years I had the privilege of working alongside Bill on a number of his international media projects and learned a great deal about trusting in God's supreme character.

In his book *God: Discover His Character*, Bill wrote these profound words: "God is sovereignly involved in directing each of our lives. Proverbs states, 'Many are the plans in a man's heart, but it is the Lord's purpose that prevails.' God carefully supervises all that happens. No event escapes his notice. No person is beyond his influence. No circumstance exists outside his control."[1]

I find tremendous hope and comfort in knowing that every breath we take and every circumstance we encounter is guided by our Wise Supervisor, God. When we're bogged down in a lengthy wait, it helps to acknowledge that God is overseeing our maddening moments. We may anxiously fidget, but God remains unruffled and perfectly on time.

In Bible times Joshua and the people of Israel learn a difficult lesson about relying on God's perfect timing and not their own. The book of Joshua records Israel's dramatic victories over the cities of Jericho and Ai. In Joshua 6:27 we read about General Joshua's growing reputation for victory: "The LORD was with Joshua, and his fame spread throughout the land." Heard of "Stormin' Norman"? Well, Joshua is Israel's military general, often leading ambushes against their opponents. In time everyone far and wide knows about Joshua and his conquering legions.

In the beginning of Joshua 9 we discover that "all the kings west of the Jordan . . . those in the hill country, in the western foothills, and along the entire coast of the Great Sea as far as Lebanon (the kings of the Hittites, Amorites, Canaanites, Perizzites, Hivites and Jebusites)" aligned to "make war against Joshua and Israel." These fearsome national leaders are not about to let Joshua muscle his way into their kingdoms.

But the people of Gibeon, the chief city of the Hivites, about five miles northwest of Jerusalem, decide to conduct their own covert operation against Joshua and Israel. The Gibeonites send out a delegation on donkeys carrying worn-out sacks and old wineskins. The men dress in tattered clothes and patched sandals. The Gibeonites perform their best hobo imitation and carry dried-up bread in their bags.

These "destitute" travelers journey the fifteen or so miles east to Gilgal, where Joshua and Israel are camped. There the Gibeonites pitch their lie: "We have come from a distant country; make a treaty with us" (Joshua 9:6).

The men of Israel immediately question the strangers' story: "But perhaps you live near us. How then can we make a treaty with you?" (Joshua 9:7). The dusty drifters respond, "We are your servants." Then they launch into a convincing story about coming from afar because they heard reports of God's fame and how he overthrew Israel's enemies.

The Hivites from Gibeon appear humble and eager to serve under the victorious nation of Israel. All the smooth talk and compliments from these foreigners must sound sweet to Joshua and his men. Perhaps the mighty warriors let grandiose thoughts of power swell their heads. The Gibeon visitors explain that they traveled from a faraway land because of the "fame of the LORD your God" (Joshua 9:9), so maybe the Israelites confuse God's fame with their own fame. Maybe they gloat, "Countries far, far away are in awe of us and afraid to come against us. Look at these poor people. They're bowing down to serve us."

The Bible doesn't tell us exactly what the people of Israel are thinking at this point, but one thing is clear: they don't wait to check out the Hivites' story. It seems Joshua just can't wait to make a peace treaty.

Joshua 9:14 is the pivotal verse in this chapter: "The men of Israel sampled their provisions but did not inquire of the LORD."

Israel doesn't wait for God.

Oh, how that's like us at times. Why wait for God's direction when we can jump into the tempting opportunities we see before us? Who needs to check in with the Almighty when it seems obvious we must act quickly?

Joshua takes into his own hands a decision that affects his entire country. He doesn't run a thorough background check on these strangers; he just makes a covenant with them based on their impressive-sounding spiel. As leader of Israel, Joshua leans on his own understanding of the situation instead of on God's direction.

In our own times of waiting, often we neglect to talk to God about our plans because we reason that (1) he's busy with bigger priorities, (2) he's too pokey to respond, and (3) he's not interested anyway.

But if we truly comprehend that God is in control of everything, we will come to know that he's not too busy, too pokey, or disinterested in the minute details of every millisecond of our lives. Trusting in God's timely control, we can affirm the prophet Jeremiah's declaration: "I know, O LORD, that a man's life is not his own; it is not for man to direct his steps" (Jeremiah 10:23).

After Joshua's blunder, the humbled leader gains a new understanding of how important it is to wait for God's direction. Because the leaders of Israel have used God's name to seal their oath with the Hivites, Israel must honor their peace treaty. In chapter 10 we learn that five kings of the Amorites who fear Israel join forces to defeat Israel's new friends, the Gibeonites. As enemy armies surround their city, the men of Gibeon send word to ask Joshua to save them.

This time Joshua listens to God, who says of the attacking armies: "Do not be afraid of them; I have given them into your hand. Not one of them will be able to withstand you" (Joshua 10:8). With that God-given encouragement, Joshua assembles his valiant warriors. They march all night to surprise the Amorites at Gibeon.

Joshua and his men unleash a "shock and awe" attack on the Amorites and then pursue them up the road to Beth Horon, a two thousand–foot incline. Can you imagine trudging all night, nearly twenty miles, in full battle gear, only to face an uphill battle the next day? Maybe you can.

> WAITING CAN MAKE US FEEL LIKE WE'VE BEEN MARCHING ALL NIGHT ONLY TO ENCOUNTER A MOUNTAIN OF OBSTACLES AHEAD.

Waiting can make us feel like we've been marching all night only to encounter a mountain of obstacles ahead. Contending with delays and postponements can exhaust us until we just want to drop our swords and quit.

Joshua and his troops are fatigued, no doubt, but they press ahead knowing God has promised to win the battle for them. On the other side of the Beth Horon mountain pass, the God who controls the weather "hurled large hailstones down on them [the Amorites] from the sky, and more of them died from the hailstones than were killed by the swords of the Israelites" (Joshua 10:11).

But after the hailstorm, daylight is slipping away, and Joshua must still defeat five kings and their remaining soldiers. So he boldly cries out to the Creator and Manager of the sun, moon, and stars. This inspiring account shows Joshua's faith in his always in-control God:

On the day the LORD gave the Amorites over to Israel, Joshua said to the LORD in the presence of Israel:

"O sun, stand still over Gibeon,
O moon, over the Valley of Aijalon."
So the sun stood still,
and the moon stopped,
till the nation avenged itself on its enemies,

as it is written in the Book of Jashar.

The sun stopped in the middle of the sky and delayed going down about a full day. There has never been a day like it before or since, a day when the LORD listened to a man. Surely the LORD was fighting for Israel! (Joshua 10:12–14)

God directs time to literally stand still so his people can conquer their enemies. The Supreme Sovereign of the universe listens to his servant Joshua and commands the sun and moon to halt. What amazing proof that God is in control of the celestial bodies and events on earth.

I find it fascinating that even extrabiblical sources document the occurrence of one long day in world history. Records from groups as diverse as the ancient Egyptians, Babylonians, Chinese, and Aztecs, combined with today's astronomical data, verify that during the time of Joshua, the sun lingered in the skies, past its usual time of setting, for the length of nearly a full day.

With such a display of God's complete control, even of the rising and setting of the sun, I wonder how I can at times doubt that he is orchestrating the minutes, hours, and days in my life.

———————

I know, however, that I'm not alone in my misgivings about God's time management. Job, whom we considered in the last chapter, also wondered about God's command over life events—until God broke in with a firm response to his questioning.

I encourage you to read all of Job 38–41 to take in the overwhelming case for God's being in absolute charge of the universe and all it contains. Here are a few highlights of God's address to the misguided Job:

Who is this that darkens my counsel with words without knowledge? Brace yourself like a man; I will question you, and you shall answer me.

Where were you when I laid the earth's foundation? Tell me, if you understand. Who marked off its dimensions? Surely you know! Who stretched a measuring line across it? . . .

Have you entered the storehouses of the snow or seen the storehouses of the hail, which I reserve for times of trouble, for days of war and battle? What is the way to the place where the lightning is dispersed, or the place where the east winds are scattered over the earth? Who cuts a channel for the torrents of rain, and a path for the thunderstorm, to water a land where no man lives, a desert with no one in it, to satisfy a desolate wasteland and make it sprout with grass? . . .

Do you know the laws of the heavens? Can you set up God's dominion over the earth? (Job 38:1–5, 22–27, 33)

Gulp! As Joshua and Job discovered, the Lord God controls time. He can speed up time or slow it down. God is also the chief architect of the foundation of the earth and the circumference of the seas. He is the foreman of the storehouses of snow, hail, rain, and ice. He oversees the patterns of lightning and wind.

I have to agree with wise King Solomon of old: "Has anyone ever seen Anyone climb into Heaven and take charge? grab the winds and control them? gather the rains in his bucket? stake out the ends of the earth?" (Proverbs 30:4 MSG). The only one I know who fits this description is the Sovereign God Most High.

The prophet Ezekiel understood the superior control possessed by his God. Throughout the Bible the phrase "Sovereign Lord" is used almost 300 times. Ezekiel, who lived as a captive during one of the most trying times in Judah's history, is recorded calling upon his Sovereign Lord roughly 220 times—more than 70 percent of those references in the entire Bible.

While Ezekiel apparently waited as a captive most of his adult life, he kept his priorities straight. The prophet fully believed that God was in control. He knew that God was completely aware of his exiled people's ongoing wait and would free them in his perfect timing.

Is waiting holding you captive? Do you feel exiled to postponement purgatory? The other person's heart isn't changing. The savings have dwindled. A better job is not visible on the horizon. The doctors are still unsure of your underlying health problem.

Author Lewis Smedes eloquently describes our unmanageable predicament with waiting: "Waiting is our destiny as creatures who cannot by themselves bring about what they hope for. We wait in the darkness for a flame we cannot light, we wait in fear for a happy ending we cannot write. We wait for a 'not yet' that feels like a 'not ever.' Waiting is the hardest work of hope."[2]

No doubt waiting is the hardest work of hope for Lazarus's sisters. Mary and Martha hope that Jesus will arrive in time to heal their brother. Once Lazarus's death shatters that hope, the women hope that

Lazarus will rise again in eternity. As the days pass, Martha and Mary hope that Jesus will eventually come to their side. But what feels like a "not ever" is really a "not yet."

When Jesus does arrive, days later than expected, he shows his sorrowful friends a miraculous reason for his delay. Mary and Martha's "not yet" is really a "you ain't seen nothin' yet!"

> WAITING IS LIFE'S LABORATORY TO SHOW US THAT WE ARE NOT IN CONTROL, BUT GOD IS.

Some people who stand by the sisters no doubt mumble and grumble, "Oh sure, this guy comes waltzing in here now, when it's too late. He can go around opening the eyes of the blind, but he can't even show up to heal one of his closet friends!"

The reception Jesus gets from some of Mary and Martha's fellow mourners is less than welcoming. But public opinion never fazes our God on a mission. Jesus visits Lazarus's tomb and calmly commands, "Take away the stone" (John 11:39).

Worrywart Martha immediately responds to Jesus's decree, "But, Lord, . . . by this time there is a bad odor, for he has been there four days." Martha uses the old "but God" objection. But God, do you realize if we move that stone, things will stink to high heaven? But God, aren't you aware of the odorous consequences of decomposition? I mean, aloe and myrrh can only cover up so much.

At this point you can almost imagine Jesus trying to hide a chuckle. Resolutely he responds, "Did I not tell you that if you believed, you would see the glory of God?" (John 11:40).

Does the "Did I not tell you?" ring in your ears like it rings in mine? How often we doubt God's ability to control the outcome of our wait.

Just when we think our wait is a stinking, rotten mess, God reassures us, "Believe, and you will see my glory."

Waiting is life's laboratory to show us that we are not in control, but God is. Downed air-force pilot Scott O'Grady saw God's glorious control; so did Joshua and his troops. So did besieged Job and detained Ezekiel.

When it comes to orchestrating our waits, God can intervene with high-powered rescue helicopters or make the sun stand still. And he can turn our eyes toward his matchless glory.

The prophet Isaiah testified of God's magnificent nature when he wrote, "Since ancient times no one has heard, no ear has perceived, no eye has seen any God besides you, who acts on behalf of those who wait for him" (Isaiah 64:4).

Wait for the God who acts on your behalf. Wait, and he'll turn your "not yets" into something no ear has heard or eye has seen. Just wait . . . you ain't seen nothin' yet.

Bare Words

Your Trustworthy God

When a train goes through a tunnel and it gets dark,
you don't throw away your ticket and jump off.
You sit still and trust the engineer.

Corrie ten Boom

Briana Lane's car fishtails on the icy canyon road above Salt Lake City, Utah. In the middle of January in the Wasatch Mountains, a slick spot on the road catches Briana off guard, and in the space of a few seconds, her car swerves from side to side and rolls over, launching her through the windshield.

The twenty-two-year-old is rushed to the University of

Utah Health Sciences Center in Salt Lake City, where she lies in critical condition with bleeding on her brain. To save the young woman's life, doctors temporarily remove nearly half of Briana's skull, planning to reattach the bone once the swelling in Briana's brain decreases. The piece of her cranium ends up in a hospital freezer.

Briana is released from the hospital in mid-February, a month before the scheduled skull-restoring surgery. Grateful to be alive, she waits at home for four weeks with a big dent in her head where doctors stitched her scalp together over her unprotected brain. She wears a plastic street-hockey helmet during the day to prevent injury.

Just bending down causes extreme pain. When she wakes every morning, Briana finds that her brain shifts to one side during the night. But Briana's medical headache only intensifies when the hospital cancels her operation the night before the planned surgery. Because the uninsured waitress can't afford to pay for the operation she so desperately needs, the hospital wants to wait to see whether Medicaid will cover the expensive procedure. She is informed that such inquiries routinely take ninety days or more.

So Briana is forced to wait—weeks and weeks, then months and months with part of her skull on ice. Her mother, Margaret McKinney, a nurse in another part of the medical center, presses the hospital and Medicaid to declare Briana's case an emergency and figure out afterward who will pay for the procedure. Hopelessly entangled in red tape, Briana's mother pleads with the hospital: "We just want what you've taken away. Can you just give us back the skull, and we'll go on with our lives?"

After months of merely wanting her skull put back together, Briana contacts a local television station to tell her story. Almost overnight Briana's surgery is scheduled—for April 30, nearly four months after her car accident. It's not clear what finally broke the impasse, but Margaret's insurance provider decides to cover her daughter's operation and her medical bills of nearly two hundred thousand dollars. Two weeks after the surgery makes Briana whole again, Utah's Medicaid officials still hadn't determined whether her case fit their eligibility requirements.[1]

I find Briana's medical wait mind-boggling. When doctors decided to let her walk around with a major hole in her head and the insurance system deliberated for months over her case, Briana had to wait and trust that someday she'd be reunited with her skull.

As I write this I'm trying to cut through some of my own medical red tape. Remember that separated shoulder I mentioned in chapter 9? After several weeks of physical therapy, I finally saw an orthopedic surgeon who specializes in shoulders.

After making me wait in the reception room for about an hour and then wait another hour for x-rays, he yanked my shoulder around and declared, "You have adhesive capsulitis." That's the fancy name for frozen shoulder. My physical therapist and therapy technicians kept warning me, "Do your exercises. You don't want adhesive capsulitis." Well, guess what? I faithfully did my exercises, and my shoulder still locked up.

I read in various medical resources that frozen shoulder is a perplexing problem that causes "substantial frustration" for patients, physical therapists, and doctors. The kicker comes when I learn that regaining full use of the shoulder joint can take up to three and a half years, with eighteen months as the average recovery time.

Eighteen months . . . three and a half years . . . do I really need to wait that long for full recovery? At least I didn't lose half my skull. At least I'm not in the final throes of cancer like my dear dad. He waited in a nursing home hoping he could regain enough strength to make it back to his own home. He waited for the chance to drive his manly man's pickup again. Dad waited for the day he was pain free, whipping around heaven without a walker.

My father's eighty-one years kept him well schooled in waiting. I pray that I, too, can model a bit of the invaluable lessons waiting chisels into the mind and heart. Lessons like contentment, peace, and trust.

Author Kathleen Norris discovered how waiting carves indelible traits into one's very being. After living a number of years in voguish New York City, Kathleen returned to the rugged lands of her pioneer ancestors. Stumbling through her adjustment to the unforgiving landscape of western South Dakota, Kathleen wrote, "I had to stay in this place, like a scarecrow in a field, and hope for the brains to see its beauty."[22]

> AS WE WAIT, BEAUTY COMES IN THE PEOPLE WHO STAND BY US THROUGH THICK AND THIN.

Waiting is like being miles and miles from the nearest latté, standing in desolate, windblown hills and hoping to see the beauty in those surroundings. Yet even when we're hogtied by the unpredictability of waiting, somehow beauty can poke through our layers of disgust and impatience. As we wait, beauty comes in the people who stand by us through thick and thin. Beauty comes in learning to dwell on what we *do* have instead of on what we lack. Even more remarkably, waiting can forge in us a deeper trust in God. Waiting brings with it the opportunity to shift our trust in the things of this world to the One who is always trustworthy.

Through difficult years of serving King Saul while waiting to become king of Israel himself, shepherd and musician David leaned ever harder on God. The book of Psalms gives us glimpses of how David's confidence in his Good Shepherd is developed in times of waiting. In fact, the Psalms speak of trusting in God more than any other book of the Bible. Here are a few choice descriptions of God's trustworthy nature from the Psalms:

- "Those who know your name will trust in you, for you, LORD, have never forsaken those who seek you." (Psalm 9:10)

- "Trust in the LORD and do good; dwell in the land and enjoy safe pasture." (Psalm 37:3)

- "Trust in him at all times, O people; pour out your hearts to him, for God is our refuge." (Psalm 62:8)

- "I will say of the LORD, 'He is my refuge and my fortress, my God, in whom I trust.'" (Psalm 91:2)

- "The works of his hands are faithful and just; all his precepts are trustworthy." (Psalm 111:7)

I can't help but wonder if the prayers and faithfulness of David's great-grandmother Ruth planted the seeds of trust in David's heart. Perhaps Ruth's life of steady dependence on God explains why she is one of only two women to have an entire book of the Bible named after them and the only Gentile woman with this honor.

Through four short chapters we follow the unfolding story of Ruth's tenacious commitment and patience to wait—for answers to come, for situations to change, for people to help her, for good to prevail.

As the Bible reveals, Ruth is a Moabite woman who married a Jewish man named Mahlon. Mahlon, his brother Kilion, and their parents moved to Moab because of a severe famine in their country of Judah. When the sons' father dies, they look after their mother Naomi. But then Mahlon and Kilion also die. Suddenly Ruth and her sister-in-law, Orpah, (no, not Oprah!) are widows like Naomi.

Ruth 1:6 tells us, "When she [Naomi] heard in Moab that the LORD had come to the aid of his people by providing food for them,

Naomi and her daughters-in-law prepared to return home from there."
Home for Naomi is Bethlehem in Judah, but dare she expect her young
daughters-in-law to travel from their native Moab with her?

The history of Ruth's Moabite nation definitely includes some
characters and incidents of which no one would care to boast. Her
family tree is rooted in sin and family dysfunction. In Genesis 19 we first
learn of a boy named Moab who becomes "the father of the Moabites"
(v. 37). Even though little Moab grows up to father a nation, he does
not possess a prestigious pedigree. He is born of incest: genetically his
father is also his grandfather, and his mother is also his half-sister.

In the ordeal at Sodom (Genesis 19), Moab's father, Lot, struggles
with not trusting God's best plans. Even with Jehovah's two angels
standing inches away from Lot and warning him to head for the hills,
verse 16 says, "He hesitated." It seems self-sufficient Lot just can't bring
himself to fully trust in God.

One has to wonder how deep the seeds of impatience and mistrust
in God grew in the mind and heart of Lot's son. For later we read that
Moab's lineage worships the gods Chemosh and Baal of Peor. As part
of their vile, cultish religion, the king of Moab even sacrifices his own
son as part of an act of devotion to Chemosh and pleas for help to
defeat the Israelites (2 Kings 3:27). God warns Israel to stay clear of the
Moabites' foreign gods, but from time to time the people of Moab lure
Israel into idolatry (Numbers 25:1–3; 1 Kings 11:1–8).

For centuries hostilities between Israel and Moab simmer while the
balance of power seesaws as first one nation dominates the other and
then the roles switch.

Yet into the country of Moab, God-fearing Israelites Elimelech,
Naomi, and their sons move. The sons marry Moabite women—women
descended from a long line of impulsive, suspicious people. These women
learn to follow Chemosh and Baal and to distrust Israel's God.

But apparently the faith of Mahlon and his family influences Ruth. When we first meet Ruth, Orpah, and their grieving mother-in-law on the road to Judah, we discover the depth of Ruth's loyalty and trust.

Already started on their journey to Bethlehem, Naomi suddenly begs her daughters-in-law to return to their own people. Naomi reasons that she is too old to provide more sons for these young gals to marry and urges them to go back and find husbands in Moab. Disheartened at losing her husband, her two sons, and now these two women who are like daughters, Naomi moans, "The Lord's hand has gone out against me!" (Ruth 1:13).

Yet Naomi's pained plea doesn't shake Ruth's confidence in her mother-in-law or in the God she serves. When Orpah decides to return to her Moabite family, Ruth remains steadfast, literally clinging to Naomi.

Naomi tries to convince Ruth to go back with her sister-in-law, where her people and gods are, but Ruth replies, "Don't urge me to leave you or to turn back from you. Where you go I will go, and where you stay I will stay. Your people will be my people and your God my Go" (Ruth 1:15–16).

Talk about a pledge of loyal commitment. Ruth loves and trusts Naomi, and Ruth loves and trusts Naomi's God. Perhaps the childless widow Ruth trusts that life will improve in the unfamiliar land of Judah. Perhaps she trusts that Israel's God will provide as he did when he led Naomi's ancestors out of Egypt.

The book of Ruth is an inspiring story of a resolute woman who waits through the loss of a husband, the loss of her own family, the loss of her culture, and the loss of her homeland. Once she arrives in her new country, Ruth waits to glean remnants of barley from the harvested fields so she and Naomi have food to eat. She waits for Boaz, a distant relative of her late husband, to claim her as his bride.

Notice that when Boaz first meets Ruth, he immediately perceives her admirable character, demonstrated in her caring for Naomi. He tells Ruth, "May the LORD repay you for what you have done. May you be richly rewarded by the LORD, the God of Israel, under whose wings you have come to take refuge" (Ruth 2:12).

Generations later, David, great-grandson of Ruth and Boaz, repeats their theme of trusting in God for refuge when he says, "How priceless is your unfailing love! Both high and low among men find refuge in the shadow of your wings" (Psalm 36:7).

Ruth, of lowly Moabite descent, depended on the one true God who, in time, lifted her to the high stature of contributing to the Davidic bloodline. Jesus Christ, the Messiah, was a descendant of King David and of his faithful great-grandmother Ruth (Matthew 1). By forsaking a centuries-old pattern of impatience and mistrust, Ruth contributed to the most important events in world history.

In the real-life classroom of waiting, Ruth learned to trust God—and so can we. One of England's most stirring preachers, Charles H. Spurgeon, once declared, "Be it ours, when we cannot see the face of God, to trust under the shadow of his wings."[3] Ruth did not directly see the face of God, but it seems she felt secure under his wings.

The television series *Joan of Arcadia* featured a high-school student, Joan Girardi, who believes she sees the face of God in various human shapes and sizes. One day Joan talks with God in the form of a cafeteria lunch lady, the next day as a dogwalker. The pilot episode set the stage for Joan's running into God in everyday life. While riding a bus to school, Joan notices a handsome, dark-haired young man smiling at her. Joan grins shyly.

After getting off the bus across from Joan's school, the cute guy follows Joan and walks up beside her. The clean-shaven teen, dressed in a T-shirt, jeans, zippered hoodie, and fleece-lined jacket, makes small talk as they head toward the school. Joan introduces herself, but the young man hesitates to disclose his name.

As the pair walks up the concrete ramp to the school, Joan's charming escort rattles off a catalog of personal information about Joan and her family and then confides that he is God. To back up his claim, he includes that she likes salt on cantaloupe and is afraid of clowns.

Stunned and somewhat frightened that this strange dude knows so many intimate details of her life, Joan snarls, "Don't ever talk to me again!" She then marches off to class while the boy just leans against a pillar, hands in his pockets.

> BY FORSAKING A CENTURIES-OLD PATTERN OF IMPATIENCE AND MISTRUST, RUTH CONTRIBUTED TO THE MOST IMPORTANT EVENTS IN WORLD HISTORY.

As Joan is leaving school, she sees the same guy waiting for her. "Hey, God, get lost! I mean it!" Joan snaps as she walks past him. He follows, so Joan threatens to turn in his description to her father, the chief of police.

"Maybe he'll be too busy thinking of creative ways to ground you for mouthing off in French class," the young man calmly replies.

Joan smirks and looks at the handsome stranger walking beside her. "Are you spying on me?"

"I'm omniscient, Joan. It comes with the job," he answers.

At that Joan stops and faces this unusual teen. "OK, so you're God."

He quickly nods his head. "Yes."

Joan rolls her eyes upward. "As in God . . ."

"Right."

"Old Testament, Tower of Babel, Burning Bush, Ten Commandments . . . God," Joan retorts.

"Well, I come off a little friendlier in the New Testament . . . but yeah, same God," explains the confident teen. The two banter as they walk across campus.

"OK, so let's say you're God," Joan finally blurts out.

"Thank you-u-u-u!"

"I want to ask you some questions," Joan continues.

"No."

"No?" Joan chirps in disbelief.

"No. As a general rule I ask questions," the teen says matter-of-factly.

Shocked at his straightforward answer, Joan says, "Are you . . . are you being snippy with me? God is snippy?"

"Let me explain something to you, Joan. It goes like this. I don't look like this; I don't look like anything you'd recognize. You can't see me . . ." the bold young man stops and faces Joan. "I take this form because you're comfortable with it. It makes sense to you. And if I'm snippy, it's because you understand snippy. You get it?"

Joan scrunches up her face. "Sort of."

"Good, because I'm really not snippy," he confides as they keep walking. "I've got a great personality. You'd like me."[4]

God does have a great personality, but sometimes when we have to wait, we're a little like Joan of Arcadia. We don't recognize God walking right by our side. We confuse him with some humans we know, so we don't trust him.

Or we consider God a stranger who's oblivious to our frustrating delays. If the waiting continues, we may even start to view God as some unfriendly, bush-burning deity who can be a bit snippy. We certainly don't consider him snappy.

Waiting tempts us to lose faith in a God who won't operate at our speed or won't jump through our hoops. But as writer and painter Basil King explained, "When you cannot trust God you cannot trust anything."[5] Ponder that one a minute. The only way we can truly trust our spouse, our kids, our friends, our in-laws, and our politicians is if we trust God first?

Maybe that's why Ruth's great-great-grandson Solomon advised, "Trust in the LORD with all your heart and lean not on your own understanding" (Proverbs 3:5). Or, as *The Message* puts it, "Trust GOD from the bottom of your heart; don't try to figure out everything on your own."

> WAITING TEMPTS US TO LOSE FAITH IN A GOD WHO WON'T OPERATE AT OUR SPEED OR WON'T JUMP THROUGH OUR HOOPS.

Trying to figure out why we need to wait and how to keep from bogging down or giving up while we wait is one way we can start mistrusting God. We think our fast-paced ways make more sense than God's methodical timing. We reason that we can trust our own judgments, our own abilities, our own plans.

But if we can't trust the most trustworthy caretaker of our mind, body, and soul, then whom can we trust? Placing our confidence in someone means we believe in that person's ability to back up words with action. We trust someone based on his or her track record of staying true to both words and behavior.

Some people choose to trust money, personal power, and luck over God. That's nothing new. The Bible talked about such people ages ago:

"Some trust in chariots and some in horses, but we trust in the name of the LORD our God" (Psalm 20:7).

But the Bible also talks about people like the royal official from Capernaum who, in his waiting for a miracle, chooses to rely on Jesus. The apostle John chronicles the plight of this concerned father with a deathly ill son.

After Jesus performs his first miracle of turning water into wine at a wedding in Cana of Galilee, word begins to spread about his divine power. Since Capernaum is only about twenty miles from Cana, perhaps the official, with access to royal transportation, attended the wedding himself.

What we know for certain is recorded in John 4:47. "When this man heard that Jesus had arrived in Galilee from Judea, he went to him and begged him to come and heal his son, who was close to death." The nobleman doesn't just politely ask Jesus for a helping hand. According to the Greek word for *begged*, this high-ranking man relentlessly pleads for Jesus to spare his son's life.

Waiting for a medical miracle can drive a person to desperation. Just ask Briana Lane. Or remember Mary and Martha's experience recorded in John 11.

Desperate to find a miraculous cure for his son before it is too late, the distressed father from Capernaum has little time to waste. He runs straight to Jesus. Notice the Master Physician's bare-bones response: "Jesus simply replied, 'Go home. Your son lives'" (John 4:50 MSG). Yet that same verse tells us, "The man believed the bare word Jesus spoke and headed home." The government official takes Jesus at his "bare word." That's complete trust.

That father returns to his family believing—without physical evidence—that Jesus will follow through on his promise. These are not the actions of a person who thinks God is some snippy stranger who simply burns bushes and livens up wedding parties.

True to his word, Jesus rewards the humble father's trust by restoring his son to health. Witnessing this incredible miracle after their scary time of fearful waiting, the official and "all his household believed" (John 4:53). They had faith that Jesus's actions would match his words. They trusted Jesus at a distance, sight unseen.

As my pastor says, "It's always about trust with God." Will we trust God to handle the details in our lives, each minute we encounter in every day? Will we trust God's timing for this day and for tomorrow?

Perhaps it's time . . . right now . . . to take God at his bare word.

Behind the Scenes

Your At-Work God

Give God his glory by resting in him, by trusting
him fully, by waiting patiently for him. This patience
honours [sic] him greatly; it leaves him, as God on the
throne, to do his work. . . . It lets God be God.

Andrew Murray

Wednesday, July 24, 2002, seems like any ordinary evening
for the miners working a mile and a half underground in the
Quecreek coal mine outside Somerset, Pennsylvania. About
two hours southeast of Pittsburgh, Somerset is a small town
nestled in the southwestern Pennsylvania coal fields. And on
a fine summer's evening, the hardworking folks of this sleepy

community never suspect that clamoring media crews will descend upon them, thrusting the area's rolling hills, dotted with cow pastures and cornfields, into the national spotlight.

Around nine o'clock, in the Quecreek mine, Mark Popernack directs an earth-devouring miner machine into a coal seam for one final slice before moving to another area. Teamed with eight other miners in that shaft, Mark has no idea that his pulverizing tear into the ancient black rock will make the national news.

The sixty-ton buzz-sawing tractor rips a six-foot-wide gash into the seam—and through the wall of an abandoned mine they don't know is there. According to an official mining map, this Saxman mine, last active in the early 1960s, is still about three hundred feet ahead.

This forsaken mine, comprised of seven miles of underground tunnels and chambers, had filled with water. With one swipe of the mining machine's cutter head, seventy million gallons of a massive underground lake suddenly pour into the Quecreek. Mark and his work buddies find themselves immersed in a raging river of frigid water blackened with coal and dirt.

Stunned and uncertain of the magnitude of their dangerous situation, the crew uses a nearby phone to warn another nine-man crew lower down in the mine: "Get out now!" Those men battle their way out of the mine through a torrent of waist-high water. Mark and his teammates are not that fortunate.

At times, dragged under the rapidly rising water, the nine miners crawl and claw their way through underground passages, many only four feet high in places. Several hours later they finally reach a high point about 240 feet from daylight. Because the floodwater has choked off the mine's ventilation system, stifling, heavy air compromises the men's breathing. Several men, their chests heaving and limbs weakened from exertion in the cold water, seek secluded spots to vomit.

Unaware that above ground more than one hundred rescuers are working feverishly to determine the best plan to free the trapped men, these shivering, frightened miners vacillate between hope and despair.

Early Thursday morning the men see their first hopeful sign. Rescuers on the surface drill a six-inch hole into the mine. Using a miners' Morse code, they bang on the drill bit extending through the hole to signal that they are alive, and the rescuers bang back that they have received the message. No one above ground is certain how many of the nine men below are still alive.

Rescuers lower a tube into the cavern through which to deliver oxygen-rich, heated air. Now able to breathe more freely, the miners no longer fear suffocating; but drowning remains a constant threat. When they hear the sound of water pumps, their optimism grows slightly. If only the pumps can drop the water faster than the underground lake spews into the deep caverns of the mine.

Meanwhile, the men's families huddle in a local firehouse and wrestle with their own fears, not knowing if their loved ones are dead or alive. The mine spokespeople present sparse and often confusing updates. Few of the on-edge family members find sleep, but tears flow freely.

"It was kind of hard to fill in the time because, you know, waiting and waiting is really a hard thing," reflects Sue Unger, whose husband, John, was trapped in the flooded mine. "But as soon as someone would walk in, the room would get real quiet, and everyone kind of sat on the edge of their seats, waiting to hear what was happening."

In the mine, at 11:45 a.m. on Thursday, Blaine Mayhugh borrows Randy Fogle's pen to write a farewell note to his family on a soggy piece of a cardboard box. Blaine then passes the pen to his father-in-law. Tom Foy and the other miners follow suit: Dennis Hall, Ron Hileman, Bob Phillippi, Mark Popernack, Bob Pugh, and John Unger. The men tuck the notes inside a plastic bucket, seal it with electrical tape, and wire it to a bolter machine at the highest part of the cavern.

With the dark pool of water now only thirty feet from them, the men make their final preparations for death. They talk about drowning with dignity and recite the Lord's Prayer together. They wait in their cheerless cubbyhole for the inevitable to happen.

At about 7:30 p.m., almost a full day after the accident, rescue workers begin drilling a twenty-nine-inch wide rescue hole through the solid limestone. A high-powered drilling rig arrives from West Virginia and slowly churns down into the rock-hard earth above the trapped men.

Huddling together to keep warm, the miners drift in and out of sleep, their teeth chattering. That night they hear the hopeful sound of drilling above them, but before long their hopes of being rescued wane. The sound stops.

At about two o'clock Friday morning, almost halfway down to the men, the fifteen-hundred-pound drill bit snaps off. A crane will need to hoist the lodged bit from its resting place 110 feet underground before workers can install a new bit. To make matters worse, the odd break in the drill bit will require the designing of a special tool to grab the bit. This process can take days, even weeks.

The drill's silence crushes the miners' morale. Growing colder and weaker by the minute, they do notice a slight drop in the water level. Or are they hallucinating?

Another drilling rig, shipped in from Ohio, has already dug a hole about a half mile from the main rescue site to drain water from the mine. This rig is then called to start drilling a second rescue hole early Friday evening.

The distressing absence of a working drill stretches to nearly eighteen hours. For three-quarters of a day, time seems to stand still. Finally, workers resume drilling and rip away at the 240 feet of solid rock. After more than three days of frantic activity, the drill bit punches through the mine ceiling just a few yards from the trapped miners.

Early Sunday morning, after seventy-seven harrowing hours of waiting, one miner after another is hauled in a metal rescue capsule to the earth's surface. After emerging from their underground tomb, the nine men are whisked away to hospitals and into the arms of their nerve-frayed families and friends.

Only later did anyone realize the saving grace of the eighteen-hour delay. While the drills were stopped, dozens of pumps worked to drain the flooded mine. According to Pennsylvania's Department of Environmental Protection, if the drill had pierced the mine's ceiling any sooner, the delicate air bubble keeping the miners alive almost certainly would have burst, allowing the water to rush in and drown them. The delay actually saved the men's lives.

Looking back on his near-death experience, miner Randy Fogle recalls how he longed to see the sun come up. Later recovering in the hospital, the third-generation coal miner still couldn't see the sunrise. His first morning at home, Randy sat out on a bench by his garage and eagerly waited for the sun to peek over the horizon.

"I wanted to watch the sun come up. It's something I thought I might never see again. Just that little thing, I mean, it happens every day," Randy says. "But when you're down in the darkness for a while, and you don't know if you're ever going to get out—well, you realize that little thing that happens every day, just the sun rising up over that hill, that's what it's all about."[1]

Many times, enduring a wait feels like you're huddled in the clammy darkness, longing for the sun to shine again. But as nineteenth-century American poet Celia Thaxter advised, "Sad soul, take comfort, nor forget / That sunrise never failed us yet."[2]

Sometimes, as for the nine Quecreek miners, a delay in seeing the sunshine or fixing a broken bit is well worth the wait. This is true even if, as we wait in agony, we can't fathom any possible positive outcome waiting for us on the other side.

Delays intrude on our jam-packed schedules. We bristle. Delays force us to slow down. We grit our teeth. Delays push us beyond our familiar, predictable world into the universe of the unknown. We grouse.

I chuckle at how author John Ortberg described our hyperactivity in waiting: "For good reasons, God does not always move at our frantic pace. We are often double espresso followers of a decaf Sovereign."[3]

A bit jittery, we can't see what God is up to through our time obstructions. But God is always up to something, often behind the scenes, for our long-term good. He reminds us of this in the Bible, his love letter to us:

Meanwhile, the moment we get tired in the waiting, God's Spirit is right alongside helping us along. If we don't know how or what to pray, it doesn't matter. He does our praying in and for us, making prayer out of our wordless sighs, our aching groans. He knows us far better than we know ourselves, knows our pregnant condition, and keeps us present before God. That's why we can be so sure that every detail in our lives of love for God is worked into something good. (Romans 8:26–28 MSG)

As we grow weary of waiting, we may fumble for words to pray. That's OK. God interprets "our wordless sighs, our aching groans." He knows our condition every millisecond and is working "something good" on our behalf. Sometimes I wonder what went through the minds of Jesus's followers as their Messiah lay entombed like a mummy. In their crushing grief and distress, I doubt they thought God was up to something good.

Jesus informed his disciples and friends that he would "be killed and on the third day be raised to life" (Matthew 16:21; Luke 9:22). But this talk of death must have seemed strange and made little sense to his supporters.

All four Gospels describe Jesus's crucifixion and burial, but no mention is made of Christ's disciples in his final moments. It's not that these men didn't care what happened to their leader. Frankly, they probably were scared to death that they'd be next on the hit list. They must have worried, *We were Jesus's closest associates—what if the chief priests, scribes, and elders want us dead too? We left our jobs and families to follow Jesus. Now what?*

When Jesus gasps for his last breath on the cross, many of the women who have followed him remain at a distance to watch as Jesus sheds his final drops of blood. A few of these women venture to Jesus's tomb two days later to anoint his body with spices.

After Jesus's death we find the disciples hiding out together in Jerusalem "with the doors locked for fear of the Jews" (John 20:19). These men and a few other close supporters share deep sadness over their beloved friend's death. But while the Messiah's loved ones mourn, he isn't just napping in the tomb.

Jesus is sealed in the grave on Friday evening. I suppose he could have come back to life the very next day. But God's Son waits two days longer. On Sunday he rises from the dead, leaving his burial linens in a neat little pile (John 20:6–7). (Isn't that just like God to tidy up after himself?) The Bible doesn't spell out every detail of how God's Son spends his hours after burial, but while his followers rest on the Sabbath, Jesus does not.

Biblical scholars wrangle about what precisely Jesus did when he, according to the Apostles' Creed, "descended into hell." But we can be certain he was up to something good. "What does 'he ascended' mean except that he also descended to the lower, earthly regions?" (Ephesians 4:9).

Some say Christ preached to the fallen angels in a holding cell in the nether world. The apostle Peter wrote, "Christ died for sins once for all, the righteous for the unrighteous, to bring you to God. He was put to death in the body but made alive by the Spirit, through whom also he went and preached to the spirits in prison who disobeyed long ago" (1 Peter 3:18–20). Others say he made ol' Satan shake in his boots. John, the disciple closest to Jesus, wrote, "The reason the Son of God appeared was to destroy the devil's work" (1 John 3:8).

Respected Bible teacher and seminary chancellor Chuck Swindoll gives a succinct overview of Jesus's activities while the Messiah's accusers rejoice and his friends grieve: "After Christ died and his body was placed in the grave, his spirit descended into the bowels of the earth. . . . There he proclaimed his victory over death, over sin, and over the power of Satan. This proclamation caused the demons to realize that their work had been in vain, and that all of their attempts to sabotage our salvation through the Cross were nullified."[4]

Jesus has some big-picture business to wrap up—business that will alter the course of every human who has ever lived. Business on which life and death hinge. In a way, Jesus steps over onto Satan's turf and declares, "I rule! I told you so." Jesus remains dead and wins the major victory over the devil, man's longtime nemesis.

From Friday night through Sunday morning, those on earth who know Jesus best give up hope that they will ever see his face again.

Mary and Martha must have felt the same way when Lazarus died. Jesus was nowhere to be found. All his promises of love and protection, presence and power, felt like distant memories or cruel jokes. The sting of death made Mary and Martha wince. Peter too.

In that tightly closed room in Jerusalem, Peter probably sobs the hardest, in spite of his typical in-control demeanor. A bit impetuous at times, Peter is the one who sliced off the servant's ear when Jesus was arrested. As one of the Christ's inner circle, Peter once boasted that he would die rather than deny Jesus. But before the rooster could crow, as Jesus had predicted, Peter was down for the count, leveled by his own reluctance to speak up for his Master.

The guilt and shame of forsaking his Lord devastates Peter and rattles his self-image of strength, devotion, and self-sufficiency. That's why I love that God makes a special point of reaching out to Peter on that original Easter Sunday. The angel at the empty tomb gives specific instructions concerning Peter to the women who first discover that Jesus is no longer in the grave: "You are looking for Jesus the Nazarene, who was crucified. He has risen! He is not here. See the place

> THE STING OF DEATH MADE MARY AND MARTHA WINCE. PETER TOO.

where they laid him. But go, tell his disciples and Peter, 'He is going ahead of you into Galilee. There you will see him, just as he told you'" (Mark 16:6–7).

Notice the "and Peter." Jesus directs the angel to send out an all-points bulletin for Peter.

The women dash off to tell the disciples that Jesus has risen from the dead. But we read that "they did not believe the women, because their words seemed to them like nonsense. Peter, however, got up and ran to the tomb" (Luke 24:11–12). Haunted by Jesus's death, Peter can't wait to see if his Lord is indeed alive. Like us, Peter is about to learn that delays are often for our good.

Behind the scenes, Jesus doesn't waste time. He perfectly times emerging from the graveyard and checking in on Peter and his friends—

just as he perfectly timed setting out to console the sisters of Bethany. Jesus explains to his disciples his delay at the Jordan River: "Lazarus died. And I am glad for your sakes that I wasn't there. You're about to be given new grounds for believing" (John 11:14–15 MSG). Raising Lazarus from the dead certainly changes the disciples' and Mary and Martha's grounds for believing in Jesus the Messiah. So does Jesus's own resurrection.

Jesus kept his word. He said he'd come back to life on the third day. Not the first day. His perfect work takes two days longer.

The Son of God used those days after his burial to triumph over Satan and work a greater good, not just for his disciples but for you and for me. Jesus defeated death, and if we believe in him, death will not conquer us. He promised: "I tell you the truth, whoever hears my word and believes him who sent me has eternal life and will not be condemned; he has crossed over from death to life" (John 5:24).

What do you think God is doing behind the scenes of your delays right now? What good could God be up to in your life and in the lives of those you love? What "new grounds" (John 11:15 MSG) is he giving you for believing him? Hold on: the best is yet to come.

A few months before Mike Yaconelli—pastor, author, and cofounder of Youth Specialties—died in a car accident, I interviewed him over the telephone. Talking with notoriously wild-and-crazy Mike refreshed my faith in our God who graciously loves us in spite of our imperfect ways. Mike's book *Messy Christianity* is on my all-time favorites list. In the chapter titled "Unspiritual Growth," Mike poignantly related how getting stuck can often be the best thing that can happen to us:

> Getting stuck is a great moment, a summons, a call from within, the glorious music of disaffection and dissatisfaction with our place in life. We get stuck when we want to change but can't,

when we want to stop destructive behavior but don't, when the tug-of-war between God's will and ours stands still and we can't move. We're stuck going nowhere, unable to get beyond a particular point.

Getting stuck can be the best thing that could happen to us, because it forces us to stop. It halts the momentum of our lives. We have no choice but to notice what is around us, and we end up searching for Jesus. When we're stuck, we're much more likely to pay attention to our hunger for God and the longings and yearnings we have stifled. Sometimes being stuck is the low point and we say, "Okay, I give up." We cannot grow without first giving up and letting go. Getting stuck forces us to see the futility of our situation and to put life in perspective so that we can move on.[5]

Mary and Martha got stuck. So did Peter. They clashed with God in a tug of war but couldn't move. The momentum of their lives halted. At their lowest points they let go of their own wills and searched for Jesus. And he showed up right on time!

Noted theologian Andrew Murray said, "We may be sure that God is never and nowhere to be found but in his ways. And that there, by the soul who seeks and patiently waits, he is always most surely to be found."[6]

As you seek and wait, rest assured that God will "always most surely be found." God, who is not confined by time, will eventually step away from the river. As with Mary, Martha, and Peter, he will show himself to you in moments—and in ways—you least expect.

God may even nudge you as you read the following account of a legendary racehorse. On Saturday, June 6, 1998, millions of people worldwide cheer for Real Quiet to gallop into history as the first

Triple Crown winner in twenty years. Having already won the coveted Preakness and the Kentucky Derby titles, the three-year-old colt looks to become the twelfth Triple Crown winner and the first since Affirmed captured the honor in 1978.

Three-eighths of a mile from home on the Belmont track, Real Quiet shifts from sixth position to first with a three-wide burst at the far turn. Real Quiet, the colt they call "The Fish," sails down the stretch, bringing the near-record crowd of 80,162 spectators scrambling to their feet. With an eighth of a mile to go, The Fish leads the pack at six lengths.

Suddenly, sleek rival Victory Gallop, who finished second to Real Quiet in the Preakness and Derby, bolts through an opening. The Fish flounders. Surging forward, chest muscles rippling, Victory Gallop appears to nip Real Quiet by a fraction of a nose at the wire. Or does he?

THOUGH HE TRIES TO APPEAR UNSHAKEN, HIS LITTLE GIRL SENSES HER FATHER'S PAIN.

The two supercharged stallions are clocked in the closest photo-finish ending in Triple Crown history. Race fans and bookies grow restless waiting for the verdict. Anxious owners pace in their boxes. Real Quiet's world-class trainer, Bob Baffert, stands to win a $5.6 million bonus if his horse wins the third jewel of the Crown.

Baffert holds his little daughter, Savannah, and waits with the rest of the world for the suspense to end. Despite silent prayers and crossed fingers, Victory Gallop edges out Real Quiet by mere inches.

A dramatic turn of fortune punctures Baffert's long-held dream. Though he tries to appear unshaken by the disheartening loss, his little girl senses her father's pain. Savannah squeezes her papa's cheeks and reassures him, "But, Daddy, you still have me!"[7]

When fortunes change and disappointments shake us, when dreams are delayed—maybe even derailed forever—it's crucial to remember that we still have God. The God who . . .

> *Sees when we stumble blindly.*
> *Embraces us with compassion.*
> *Loves us even when we're a long way off.*
> *Gives us strong shoes for the stony paths of waiting.*
> *Lifts us gently when we are cast down.*
> *Fills our empty hands with gifts of tender mercy.*
> *Understands everything even when we're clueless.*
> *Extends patience even when we grumble.*
> *Settles us with his perfect peace.*
> *Comforts us by just being there.*
> *Controls all of life's details.*
> *Proves completely trustworthy.*
> *Works behind the scenes, transforming delays into*
> *   something good.*

Centuries ago the prophet Isaiah called his people to deeper faith. He waited decades for his countrymen to learn to rest in the riches of knowing God more fully. The prophet proclaimed: "Yes, LORD, walking in the way of your laws, we wait for you; your name and renown are the desire of our hearts" (Isaiah 26:8).

Though life is full of delays, God is always at work. He longs for you to delight in him. He waits for you to discover new grounds for trusting him.

What are you waiting for?

Questions for Reflection

Chapter 1. Lingering by the River: *Your Timely God*

1. Describe a season of delay in your own life. What is it like to wait on the God of the universe?

2. How does today's culture influence your expectations of waiting?

3. When you are made to wait, what doubts surface about God's character?

4. In what ways do you feel that God is lingering by the river (in your life . . . in your nation . . . in our world)?

5. What are common "but God" complaints you lodge when you worry that you're about to "die in the desert"?

6. How can you be more consistent in viewing God "on the other hand"—for instance, seeing him as loving, faithful, all-powerful, and timely?

7. In what areas do you need "to be given new grounds for believing" (John 11:15 MSG)?

8. Read Isaiah 41:17–20. Perhaps, in waiting, you feel "poor and needy" or "parched with thirst." What would it take for you to consider and understand that the Holy One wants to turn your desert of delays into "pools of water"?

Chapter 2. Seeing Is Believing: *Your All-Seeing God*

1. What stands out to you most about the Birdwells' traumatic experience?

2. Do you agree or disagree that God kept his eye on every person and every circumstance involved in the terrible 9/11 attacks? Explain.

3. Have you ever reasoned, as Sarai might have, that desperate waiting calls for desperate measures? Has waiting ever pushed you to take matters into your own hands? Explain.

4. Do you think God views the mundane and monumental events in your life with equal concern? Explain.

5. What tempts you to believe that God is blind and indifferent to your needs?

6. In what ways are you spiritually blind to the immense character of God? What keeps you from processing what you see is true about God?

7. What specific things in your life today cloud your perception of your all-seeing God?

8. What is your greatest challenge right now in trusting that God's eyes are on you and that he sees your every step (Job 34:21)?

9. What people or circumstances prevent you from clearly hearing God's direction?

10. Read Psalm 34:15 and Proverbs 15:3. What can you apply to your life about "the eyes of the Lord"?

Chapter 3. When God Stops: *Your Compassionate God*

1. Reflect on a time when you felt you were in a "pit" in your life. Like Coolidge Winesett, did you think you had no chance of help? Explain.

2. How does waiting sometimes make you feel like a beggar pleading for God's attention?

3. What compels you these days to cry out, "How long, O Lord"?

4. What is your take on God's asking his children, "How long?" What does this say about God's patience?

5. When is it appropriate to cry out to God and beg, and when do these pleas turn into whining? Do you believe God eventually regards all of our persistent supplications as annoying chatter?

6. How does waiting involve both God and you?

7. Have you ever felt that God stopped just for you? Describe that experience.

8. What distresses you most in life? How can you be more compassionate toward yourself in these distressing times?

9. In the past when someone acted with compassion toward you, did you recognize the hand of God, or did you turn your attention to that person and forget about God's involvement in your life? Explain. How can you be more aware of God's acts of compassion toward you in the little, everyday things?

10. Read Psalm 103. What specifics from these verses add fresh insight to your understanding of God's compassion?

Chapter 4. A Long Way Off: *Your Loving God*

1. Have you ever looked for love and affirmation in the wrong places? Explain. How did God woo you back, or how is he currently wooing you back?

2. What keeps you from fully believing you are deeply loved?

3. What would you have to change to "put on love" in your everyday life as Colossians 3:14 advises?

4. In what way does God's "I love you" fall on deaf ears? How do you

identify with the movie character Ernie Hemingway's missing the connection with someone's message of love?

5. How does waiting affect the way you give and receive love?

6. In what ways might you, like the prodigal son, be squandering the gifts and blessings God has given you?

7. Have you ever felt a long way off from God? If so, describe your experience.

8. How can you accept and love someone in your life who is a long way off from God? What small step can you take this week to embrace this person with the open arms of love modeled in Luke 15?

9. Does anything in your life today interfere with your trusting God to uphold his faithful pledge of love?

10. Read Zephaniah 3:17. List all the ways in which this verse describes how God demonstrates his love for you.

Chapter 5. Strong Shoes: *Your All-Powerful God*

1. What about Jean Driscoll's story inspires you? List one thing that emboldens your spirit to dream big and work hard.

2. As you endure the blustery winds of waiting, what makes it most difficult for you to put your head down and keep going?

3. Consider a time when your life demonstrated the "when I am weak, then I am strong" truth from 2 Corinthians 12:10. Why is this truth often hard to comprehend?

4. What is the most difficult part about coming to the end of your own strength? What's the best part?

5. Put yourself in King Jehoshaphat's royal sandals. What political risk did he take in turning to God instead of to his military chiefs? How do you think a scenario like the one in 2 Chronicles 20 would play out in political circles today?

6. When you've been faint in waiting, how has God renewed your strength?

7. It's tempting to get ahead of yourself and God. How do Sam's words to Frodo, "Come on, let's just make it down the hill for starters" (from the

movie *Lord of the Rings: Return of the King*) speak to you today?

8. How can waiting stretch your belief in your all-powerful God?

9. At what stage are you on your journey? Are you sprinting to freedom, stumbling on the rocky road, or collapsing in the ditch? As God comes to your side, what empowering words do you need to hear from him?

10. Read Isaiah 33:2. Make this your prayer especially on days when you feel too weak to stand firm.

Chapter 6. Smiling in the Rain: *Your Gentle God*

1. Describe a dreary time when you really needed a brush of levity. Who are the people in your life who keep your heart smiling come rain or shine?

2. What keeps many people from viewing the Almighty as a gentle God? What keeps you from seeing him this way?

3. In the world today, what would make someone's heart shrink back from God? How would you describe the condition of your heart toward God in this season of your life?

4. Think of a time when you felt frazzled, like Elijah. How did God gently nurture you? Or if you feel that he failed to show up, explain why you feel that way.

5. What misconceptions about being gentle are fostered in our be-tough, be-aggressive culture? How has society influenced your thoughts regarding kindness and gentleness?

6. Explain why it's natural to expect God to march into your circumstances and dramatically turn the tables. Why doesn't God typically rescue his people today with supernatural feats?

7. Has God shown up as a gentle whisper in your life? If so, explain.

8. Think of someone who models God's gentleness in your life. What about this person's gentle ways would you like to emulate?

9. Think of a time when you found yourself spiritually flailing like a cast sheep. Who or what helped you get back on your feet?

10. Read Matthew 5:3 and 1 Peter 3:4. What is blessed about reflecting a "gentle and quiet spirit"?

Chapter 7. Open Hands: *Your Merciful God*

1. Have you ever thought God was like the "Soup Nazi"? Why? What in your life right now causes you to see him as temperamental and harsh?

2. Describe a time when you felt God was asking too much of you. (Remember the story of the new bride Signa marching cows across a lumpy field on her wedding night.) Has God ever felt that merciless to you?

3. Many people in the Bible boasted of God's mercy. But in this day and age, what clouds our view of God's mercy?

4. Micah 7:18 says of God: "You . . . delight to show mercy." How do you see God delighting to showing mercy today? Or do you think he's withholding his mercy in some way? Explain.

5. God doesn't necessarily expect you to be an Oscar Schindler or Winnie Babihuga. But what can you do to show that you "love mercy" (Micah 6:8)?

6. What makes it hard for you to open your hands to receive gifts of mercy? From whom can you learn when it comes to humbly receiving unmerited favor?

7. What incidents make your blood boil? Think of a time when you were closer to maniacal than merciful. What could you have done to respond in a more God-pleasing manner?

8. Mercy is not our natural human tendency. How might under-standing God's mercy toward you affect your life on a daily basis?

9. Read Psalm 28. Discuss David's plea for God's mercy for himself but no mercy for the wicked. How does God want you to respond to those who do evil?

Chapter 8. Writing in the Dirt: *Your Understanding God*

1. Describe a time when you felt like you were "on the edge of hell." What helped soothe your scorched soul?

2. When we must wait, why is it so easy to blame God? Think of at

least one person in Scripture who seemed to master that skill.

3. What character and propensities typically creep into your responses to difficult people and situations? (Go on; it's OK to admit the good, the bad, and the ugly.)

4. Do you really believe that God "gets" you? Why or why not?

5. Since Isaiah 40:28 says that "no one can fathom" God's understanding, should we even try to understand him? Explain.

6. In today's culture what makes it difficult for you to be real with people? Share both a positive and negative experience you've had while trying to be real with someone.

7. How can you become more real with God? What would that look like for you?

8. In what ways do you resemble the self-righteous Pharisees? Why is it often easier to detect someone else's faults than your own?

9. Write a prayer asking God to give you an understanding heart. Thank him for always understanding you.

10. Read Romans 8:1–6. How can these verses help free you from a spirit of condemnation toward yourself and others?

Chapter 9. Breathe Deep: *Your Patient God*

1. What are you learning from the lessons of patience that waiting produces?

2. What typically makes it hard for you to respond calmly and sensibly in trying times?

3. What part do Adam and Eve play in your human tendency toward impatience? What is your perspective on spiritual genetics and the "I was born this way" reasoning when it comes to being accountable for sin?

4. When do you grumble loudest? How does your grumbling affect the people around you?

5. How effective is muffling your grumbling before God? What are healthy ways to deal with a disgruntled heart?

6. Typically, when people believe they're right, they tend to justify their

impatience. How can self-centered thinking cause impatience?

7. Why do you think God chooses waiting as a test for you? Can you think of something else he could choose instead? What might waiting teach you that nothing else could?

8. Is there a neutral zone where you can complain about waiting without crossing into criticizing your Maker? Explain.

9. List at least two examples in both the Old and New Testaments where God kept his cool with his people. What can you learn from these examples?

10. Read Proverbs 14:29 and 15:18. List practical outcomes of countering a quick temper with patience. How can you learn to breathe deeply and integrate patience into your everyday moments? Whom can you enlist as a patience mentor?

Chapter 10. It Is Well: *Your Peaceful God*

1. How does seeing other people's faith in God inspire you to trust him too? Describe one person who inspires your faith in God today. How does this person model tranquillity in life's swirling circumstances?

2. What's it like to watch someone you love remain stuck in perpetual waiting mode? From your own life, what can you share with your loved one about how to find peace in the midst of delay?

3. Consider the world today. Where do you see the greatest stirrings of unrest and the greatest signs of peace?

4. The Israelites often were disobedient when forced to wait. What in your life now makes it difficult to obey God? What might make it easier for you to obey?

5. How can unhealthy patterns of unrest creep into our lives if we're not careful? What are practical ways to soothe our own unrest?

6. What familiar excuses have you raised to God as to why you should be exempt from life's postponements? How sharp are your bargaining skills with God?

7. When the torrential rains and shrill winds of waiting rage against you, how can you hide under God's wings?

8. Read Luke 7:36–50. Why do you think Jesus's last words to this woman were, "Go in peace"? How can you apply Jesus's words to your life?

Chapter 11. Just Being There: *Your Comforting God*

1. What sorts of things bring you comfort?

2. How do you "just be there" for someone in need? When you're struggling, what do you want someone else to do to "be there" for you? From your own experience, how would you describe a ministry of presence?

3. How do you typically respond to someone who is weary from waiting? What are some practical steps you can take to become a better listener?

4. Think of some strong people in your life who may not appear to have needs. How can you encourage them to lean on you when they need comfort and support?

5. Think of at least two people in the Bible who were OK with acknowledging to God and others that they were "a mess." What about their honesty appeals to you?

6. What are some portions of Scripture that comfort you?

7. Think of a time of waiting when you really needed to hear the voice of God. How did he answer?

8. In waiting for their grief and despair to subside, Peter and his fishing buddies went fishing. Where do you turn when you're confused and stressed by life's delays?

9. What are some signs that God may be sending you a fresh wind of comfort today?

10. Read Ruth 1:1–17, Matthew 25:35–40, and Mark 2:1–12. What does comfort look like in each of these situations? Consider how you can practice some of these forms of comfort in times of waiting.

Chapter 12. Not Yet: *Your In-Control God*

1. Try to put yourself in Scott O'Grady's boots, hiding out in enemy territory. What might you have thought about God at such a time?

2. Scott talked about how the hard times of waiting help him see God's true character. In your own times of waiting, what have you discovered to be true about God?

3. Why do humans struggle so much with control? What about our culture makes us feel the need to be in control?

4. What is your view on the relationship between God's control and man's free will? How do you reconcile God's ability to change circumstances with our own responsibility to conduct our lives?

5. How much do you feel God really wants to get involved in the specifics of your life? How much do you want him to be involved?

6. When you're waiting, what makes it difficult for you to release your grip on your life and open your hands to accept God's control?

7. What individuals do you know who consistently let God order their steps? Talk with them this week about practical ways in which they allow God to control their lives.

8. Where are you today in the battle to wait and let God be in control? Are you marching onward or ready to drop your sword? From the story in Joshua 9 and 10, what encourages you to trust that God is with you and fighting for you?

9. How are you waiting in the darkness for a flame you cannot light? What "not yet" in your life is feeling like a "not ever"?

10. Read Job 38–41. Write down the ways God is fully orchestrating all of creation. What verses from these chapters can you cling to as you believe and wait to see God's glory revealed as you wait?

Chapter 13. Bare Words: *Your Trustworthy God*

1. What invaluable lessons has waiting chiseled into your mind and heart?

2. Trace any seeds of mistrust rooted in your family's history. What are you doing in your life today to transplant seeds of trust?

3. Lot couldn't bring himself to have full confidence in God. What keeps you from fully believing God? What specific characteristics of God are you starting to trust more?

4. Describe a time when, like Naomi, you moaned, "The Lord's hand has

gone out against me" (Ruth 1:13). What made it so hard to trust God in your circumstance?

5. What do you think would happen in your life and the lives of others if you stopped being impatient and mistrusting? What are some practical steps you can take to make these changes in attitude and behavior?

6. Like Joan of Arcadia, what keeps you from recognizing God at your side?

7. On a scale of one to five (five being highest), rate God's promptness (as you perceive it) in your life. Using the same scale, rate your comfort with trusting God for your daily bread.

8. Contemplate this statement: the only way you can truly trust your spouse, your kids, your friends, your in-laws, and your politicians is if you trust God first. Do you agree or disagree? Why?

9. Think of a time when you felt that your quick solutions made more sense than God's methodical timing? How did you proceed?

10. Read Matthew 4:18–22 and 9:9. For what big and little things did Jesus's disciples need to trust him as they left everything to follow him? Read Psalm 40:4. What would it look like to truly make the Lord your trust?

Chapter 14. Behind the Scenes: *Your At-Work God*

1. Do you ever feel like a "double espresso follower of a decaf Sovereign?" When and why? In what ways do you wish God would switch to at least a full-strength latté?

2. What can make you doubt that God is always up to something for your long-term good?

3. What steals your hope of God's showing up when you need him most?

4. Describe a time when you learned that a delay truly was for your good. How did this experience change your view of God?

5. How can getting "stuck" be a good thing?

6. Do you honestly believe that the best is yet to come in your life? Explain.

7. What do you think God might be doing behind the scenes of your

current delays? If you could give God a little advice on how to work, what would you tell him?

8. Look back briefly over each chapter in this book. What new grounds do the Scriptures and anecdotes in this book give you for trusting God? How will you begin to act on what you've read?

9. Andrew Murray once wrote, "God has new developments and new resources. He can do new things, unheard-of-things, hidden things. Let us enlarge our hearts and not limit Him."[1] Read 1 Corinthians 2:9. Make a list of the unseen and unheard-of things you want God to do in your life now and in the future. How can trust in God's character influence your list?

Notes

Chapter 1. Lingering by the River: *Your Timely God*

1. Previously published in *Washington Post*, "Iraqi man holes up in wall for twenty-two years," printed in *Colorado Springs Gazette*, June 18, 2003.

Chapter 2. Seeing Is Believing: *Your All-Seeing God*

1. Richard Foster, "Deepening Our Conversation with God," *Leadership Journal* 18, no. 1 (Winter 1997): 112.

2. Nancy Keene, "Take a Deep Breath: What to Do When Your Child Is First Diagnosed," The Leukemia & Lymphoma Society, February 12, 2003, http://www.leukemia-lymphoma.org/.

3. Carol Lin, "Blind climber describes Everest adventure," June 1, 2001, http://www.cnn.com/2001/US/06/01/blind.climber.cnna/.

Chapter 3. When God Stops: *Your Compassionate God*

1. Greg Barrett, "Virginia man survives for four days in outhouse pit," *Colorado Springs Gazette*, August 27, 2000.

2. Andrew Murray, *Waiting on God* (Belfast, Northern Ireland: Ambassador Publications, 1997), 73–75.

3. *Merriam Webster's Collegiate Dictionary*, 10th ed. (Springfield, Mass.: Merriam-Webster, Inc., 1993), 234.

4. *The Pianist*, directed by Roman Polanski (Universal Studios, 2002).

5. Martin Luther King Jr., "Beyond Vietnam—A Time to Break Silence" (speech, Riverside Church, New York, NY, April 4, 1967), http://www.americanrhetoric.com/speeches/mlkatimetobreaksilence.htm (accessed September 5, 2005).

Chapter 4. A Long Way Off: *Your Loving God*

1. Mother Teresa, *The Joy in Loving*, comp., Jaya Chaliha and Edward Le Joly (New York: Penguin Books, 1997), 151.

2. Diana, Princess of Wales, interview by Martin Bashir, *Panorama*, BBC1, November 20, 1995, http://www.bbc.co.uk/politics97/Diana/panorama.html (accessed May 27, 2005).

3. *In Love and War*, directed by Richard Attenborough (New Line Cinema, 1997).

4. *Colorado Springs Gazette*, "Call her Rebound Barbie—plastic couple calls it quits," February 13, 2004.

5. Sherwood Eliot Wirt and Kersten Beckstrom, eds., *Living Quotations for Christians* (New York: Harper & Row, 1974), 92.

Chapter 5. Strong Shoes: *Your All-Powerful God*

1. Sherwood Eliot Wirt and Kersten Beckstrom, eds., *Living Quotations for Christians* (New York: Harper & Row, 1974), 4.

2. Ibid., 232.

3. *Lord of the Rings: Return of the King*, directed by Peter Jackson (New Line Cinema, 2003).

4. Marvin Harwit, review of *Birth of Infancy and Stars*, Robert Lucas, Alain Omont, and Raymond Stora, eds., *Science* 231 (March 7, 1986): 1201–2.

5. Sherwood Eliot Wirt and Kersten Beckstrom, eds., *Living Quotations for Christians* (New York: Harper & Row, 1974), 155.

6. Ibid., 66.

Chapter 6. Smiling in the Rain: *Your Gentle God*

1. Wesley D. Camp, *What a Piece of Work Is Man!: Camp's Unfamiliar Quotations from 2000 B.C. to the Present* (Englewood Cliffs, N.J.: Prentice Hall, 1990), 117.
2. Max Lucado, *In the Eye of the Storm* (Dallas: Word Publishing, 1991), 131.
3. Frank S. Mead, ed. and comp., 12,000 *Religious Quotations* (Grand Rapids: Baker Book House, 1989), 50.
4. Phillip Keller, *A Shepherd Looks at Psalm 23* (Grand Rapids: Zondervan, 1970), 60.

Chapter 7. Open Hands: *Your Merciful God*

1. Willa Cather, *O Pioneers!* (New York: Mariner Books, Houghton Mifflin Company, 1941), 132–33.
2. Wirt and Beckstrom, *Living Quotations for Christians*, 5.
3. Ibid.
4. Bill Bright, *God: Discover His Character* (Orlando: NewLife Publishers, 1999), 232–33.
5. C. S. Lewis, Letters to an American Lady (Grand Rapids: Eerdmans, 1967), 73.

Chapter 8. Writing in the Dirt: *Your Understanding God*

1. Mary Beth Brown, "Ronald Reagan's faith and his journey home," WorldNetDaily.com, June 7, 2004, http://www.worldnetdaily.com/news/article.asp?ARTICLE_ID=38817 (accessed September 7, 2005).
2. *Merriam Webster's Collegiate Dictionary*, 11th ed. (Springfield, Mass.: Merriam-Webster, Inc., 2003), 1365.
3. Margery Williams, *The Velveteen Rabbit: Or How Toys Become Real* (New York: Bantam Doubleday Dell Publishing Group, Inc., 1991), 5–8.
4. Will Englund, "Girl denied academic honor after writing letter to Putin," *Baltimore Sun*, printed in *Colorado Springs Gazette*, June 21, 2000.

Chapter 9. Breathe Deep: *Your Patient God*

1. Associated Press, "A 24,800-mile walk in sandals of straw," *Colorado Springs Gazette*, September 20, 2003.
2. Barbara Kingsolver, *The Poisonwood Bible* (New York: HarperFlamingo, 1998), 283.

3. Ibid., 30.

4. *The Columbia World of Quotations* at Bartleby.com, #41733, http://www.bartleby.com/66/33/41733.html.

5. The Virtues, "A Collection of Quotations on the Virtue of Patience," http://www.thevirtues.org/site/11-Patience.html.

6. Uncommon Courtesy & Coaching, "Motivational Quotes about Patience," http://www.uncommoncourtesy.com/patiencequotations.htm.

7. Ibid.

8. Ibid.

9. The Virtues, "A Collection of Quotations on the Virtue of Patience," http://www.thevirtues.org/site/11-Patience.html.

Chapter 10. It Is Well: *Your Peaceful God*

1. United Nations General Assembly, excerpts from the provisional verbatim record of the thirty-second meeting held at Headquarters, New York, October 23, 1990, http://www.un.org/spanish/ha/chernobyl/documentos/45pv32.htm.

2. Kay Arthur, *Lord, I Want to Know You* (Sisters, Ore.: Multnomah Books, 1992), 129.

3. Sherwood Eliot Wirt and Kersten Beckstrom, eds., *Living Quotations for Christians* (New York: Harper & Row, 1974), 170.

4. Ibid., 87.

Chapter 11. Just Being There: *Your Comforting God*

1. "The Unforgiven," *Judging Amy*, written by Karen Hall (Twentieth Century Fox Film Corporation & CBS Worldwide. Inc., April 24, 2001).

2. Sherwood Wirt and Kersten Beckstrom, eds., *Living Quotations for Christians* (New York: Harper & Row, 1974), 37.

3. Anna Quindlen, *Loud and Clear* (New York: Random House, 2004), 20.

Chapter 12. Not Yet: *Your In-Control God*

1. Bill Bright, *God: Discover His Character* (Orlando: New Life Publishers, 1999), 115.

2. Lewis B. Smedes, *Standing on the Promises* (Nashville: Thomas Nelson, 1998), 41–42.

Chapter 13. Bare Words: *Your Trustworthy God*

1. Associated Press, "Medical Headache," *Colorado Springs Gazette*, May 14, 2004.
2. Kathleen Norris, *Dakota* (New York: Houghton Mifflin Company, 1993), 3.
3. Sherwood Eliot Wirt and Kersten Beckstrom, eds., *Living Quotations for Christians* (New York: Harper & Row, 1974), 246.
4. "Pilot," *Joan of Arcadia* (Barbara Hall Productions, Inc., and CBS Productions, in association with Sony Pictures Television, September 26, 2003).
5. Wirt and Beckstrom, Living Quotations for Christians, 245.

Chapter 14. Behind the Scenes: *Your At-Work God*

1. The Quecreek Miners as told to Jeff Goodell, *Our Story: 77 Hours That Tested Our Friendship and Our Faith* (New York: Hyperion, 2002), 77–78, 176.
2. John Bartlett, comp., *Familiar Quotations*, 10th ed., Bartleby.com, #7773, http://www.bartleby.com/100/578.2.html.
3. John Ortberg, *If You Want to Walk on Water, You've Got to Get Out of the Boat* (Grand Rapids: Zondervan Publishing House, 2001), 176.
4. Charles R. Swindoll, *Hope in Hurtful Times: A Study of 1 Peter* (Fullerton, Calif.: Insight for Living, 1990), 80.
5. Mike Yaconelli, *Messy Spirituality* (Grand Rapids: Zondervan Publishing House, 2002), 92–93.
6. Andrew Murray, *Waiting on God* (Belfast, Northern Ireland: Ambassador Publications, 1997), 48.
7. Bob Baffert with Steve Haskin, *Dirt Road to the Derby* (Lexington, Ky.: The Blood Horse Group, Inc., 1999), 153.

Questions for Reflection

1. Andrew Murray, Waiting on God (Belfast, Northern Ireland: Ambassador Publications, 1997), 9.

About the Author

Beth Lueders is an award-winning journalist and founder and director of MacBeth Communications, a writing and editorial business. Her journalistic work has garnered five Evangelical Press Association (EPA) Awards. Lueders has authored, co-authored, and edited several books including the Women of Faith Study Bible and numerous others. She currently resides in Colorado Springs.